MW00908460

FATIMA AND THE TRIUMPH OF MARY
Reflections on the Fatima Message

Father Andrew Apostoli, C.F.R.

FATIMA AND THE TRIUMPH OF MARY

Reflections on the Fatima Message

Foreword by
Most Reverend Frank J. Caggiano

World Apostolate of Fatima   Washington, New Jersey

This publication was examined by a censor of the Diocese of Metuchen and has been judged acceptable in accord with Canon 827 to receive ecclesiastical approbation.

Imprimatur:
Most Reverend James F. Checchio, JCD

Nihil Obstat:
Reverend John G. Hillier, Ph.D.
Censor Librorum
June 7, 2016

N.B. Ecclesiastical permission implies that the material contained herein has been examined by diocesan censors and nothing contrary to faith and morals has been found.

Cover Art:
Fatima Apparitions
© Joe De Vito

Cover design by Megan R Pritchard

All articles were originally published in *Soul Magazine*,
the official publication of the World Apostolate of Fatima, USA.
Copyright ©2016 World Apostolate of Fatima,
P.O. Box 976, Washington, NJ 07882

ISBN: 978-0-692-73590-9
Printed in the United States of America

DEDICATION

This book is lovingly dedicated to the Blessed Virgin Mary who, in her love and care for her children on earth, appeared 100 years ago in Fatima, Portugal, to warn us of great evils that would come upon the world and how we must resist these evils by living her peace plan from heaven!

TABLE OF CONTENTS

CHAPTER EIGHT
OUR LADY OF FATIMA'S MESSAGE AND
THE SPIRITUALITY OF SAINT PADRE PIO

FOREWORD

In every age of the Church's life, faithful followers of the Lord Jesus have faced numerous and serious challenges. Discipleship is never an easy matter. Rather, it demands sacrifice, repentance, conversion, reparation for sin and a life of deep prayer and surrender to the power of the Holy Spirit.

Since the time of the apostles, countless Catholics have remained faithful to Christ despite being persecuted at the hands of the Roman Empire, being tempted to follow the false teachings of those who compromised the truth of our Catholic faith or the ways of the larger culture. Every disciple of Christ must face an inescapable choice countless times in life: either to remain faithful to Christ or become one with the world. Through the grace of the Holy Spirit, many have chosen courageously and faithfully to follow Christ. You and I must also make this same choice.

As was true in former ages, it is true in our own age. Perhaps, now more than ever, we must recognize the spiritual threats around us and respond with fidelity and courage.

What is the path that one must follow in order to persevere in faith, hope and love? The answer to this question is a simple one. It can be summarized in the message that Our Lady offered to Lucia, Jacinta and Francisco at Fatima. It is the same message being offered to you and me. It is a timely message that addresses the challenges we face and invites us to effectively live and preach the Gospel of life and joy. Our Lady of Fatima provides us a recipe for spiritual renewal, rooted in penance, prayer, sacrifice, reparation for sin and intercessory prayer for ourselves and for sinners throughout the world. It is a message beautifully and powerfully outlined in the essays that comprise this spiritually insightful book.

It should not be a surprise that Our Lady's appearance at Fatima was given to us as a great grace at the dawn of our modern age. From the last moments of the Lord's earthly life, while dying on the cross, Christ Jesus gave to you and me a spiritual mother - an advocate, guide and protector - who always walks with the Church, urging us to rediscover her Son and to love Him as she does. As Venerable Archbishop Fulton Sheen once noted, just as the moon does not shine with its own light but in the darkness of the night reflects the light of the hidden sun, so too has our Lady shone through the darkness of every age, reflecting the light of her Son to a world that often found itself in growing darkness.

Just as a mariner looks to the moon for direction in times of both tranquil and turbulent travel, so too do we who journey through life in this modern age have the light of Our Lady of Fatima to lead us.

The message of Fatima was given to a world that has faced war, violence and terror. Her message gives encouragement to the Church that continues to suffer persecution and even martyrdom because it remains faithful to her Son who is "the Way the Truth and the Life" (Jn 14:6).

The message of Fatima offers a way out of war, violence and sin. Our Lady asked for conversion, penance, reparation and sacrifice in light of our personal sins. Such conversion will help unmask the culture of death and counter the widespread spirit of secularism that continues to weaken our families, neighborhoods and even our communities of faith. Her revelation of the vision of hell to the young visionaries added a sense of great urgency to the need for conversion, in light of the spirit of indifference that grips our society. It is this attitude of indifference that blocks many from hearing the Gospel message of hope, joy and peace that comes from the Lord Jesus. The message of Our Lady of Fatima gently but firmly challenges those enslaved by an attitude of indifference to look beyond themselves and, by embracing a path of penance and conversion, to seek the destiny that awaits them in Christ.

Through his many spiritual insights, Father Andrew Apostoli provides his readers with invaluable lessons that illustrate the richness of Our Lady's message at Fatima. His analyses of the challenges we face in our contemporary world are both honest and direct. While explaining the many dimensions of Our Lady's message, Father Apostoli also provides clear summaries of many of our Church's dogmatic beliefs, oftentimes misunderstood by many Catholics. Just as when we encounter a beautiful painting and stand before it, reflecting upon the insights that it conveys, this book brings us before the events of Fatima and offers us the opportunity to learn from Our Lady at Fatima what it is that you and I must do to remain faithful to her Son.

As I read this book, I recalled the example of my own mother. I was blessed to have a mother whose tireless devotion to Our Lady helped me as a little boy to grow in love and devotion to Mary, the Mother of God. My mother's love for our Blessed Mother only grew stronger in the final months of her life, as she struggled with the growing debilitation of lung cancer.

One of my mother's final requests was to visit the shrine of Our Lady of Fatima, which we did a few months before she died. Upon our arrival, notwithstanding her exhaustion from the flight and the debilitating effects of chemotherapy, my mother insisted that we participate in that evening's candlelight procession. Soon after we returned to the hotel that evening, with a look of deep peace and joy, I will never forget the words that my mother said to me. From her seat near her bed, holding the rosary beads that she used during the procession, she whispered softly: "Tonight I saw a glimpse of what Heaven will be like."

Through the intercession of the Immaculate Heart of Mary, may all who read this book and follow the message of Our Lady of Fatima one day have the grace to see and enter fully into the glory of Heaven.

Most Reverend Frank J. Caggiano
Bishop of Bridgeport

Author's Preface

Of all the great apparitions of Our Lady in more recent centuries, those of Fatima stand out as probably the most urgent and important of them. All of them have had great consequences for the Church in the world. At Guadalupe in 1531, Our Lady's apparitions to St. Juan Diego led to the conversion of nearly 10 million native peoples, Aztec and Mayan Indians. She is called the Queen of the Americas, the Star of Evangelization and the Protectress of the Unborn. At Lourdes in France Our Lady appeared in 1858 to St. Bernadette to provide spiritual strength as well as bodily healing for millions. At Fatima in 1917, Our Lady warned the world of terrible wars and the spread of the evil of Communism that would bring much suffering upon the world and great persecution for the Catholic Church. As I write this preface, we do not know exactly when or how the final fulfillment of Our Lady's promise will actually come, but when it does it will bring with it Her Triumph leading to world peace through the salvation of souls.

For more than 10 years, I have been writing articles for *Soul Magazine*, a publication of the World Apostolate of Fatima USA. It is dedicated to promoting the message of Our Lady of Fatima, so needed in the world today. This book contains a number of those articles related to Fatima. My hope is that it will help people prepare themselves with greater knowledge and love for the centenary celebrations of the Angel of Peace apparitions (in 2016) and those of Our Lady of Fatima (in 2017) to the three young shepherd children who were the visionaries that were given this great peace plan from Heaven: Lucia dos Santos, aged 10; Francisco Marto aged 9 and his little sister Jacinta Marto aged 7.

Many people are amazed to learn a lot of the details that are generally not known about the Fatima story. It then helps them to appreciate the message in a deeper way and hopefully to respond more fully to what Our Lady has requested. Remember, Our Lady had told Lucia, "When enough people do as I have requested, my Triumph will come and that will bring peace into the world!"

It is my hope that this book will help many people become what Pope Emeritus Benedict XVI called "apostles of Our Lady of Fatima!" This requires three things: "Learn the message of Fatima, live the message of Fatima and spread the message of Fatima!" Let us all be resolved to do all we can to help bring on the Triumph of our Lady of Fatima! The future of the world will depend on it!

Acknowledgments

I would first like to thank Mr. David Carollo, the Executive Director of the World Apostolate of Fatima - USA (also called the "Blue Army") for publishing this book. He certainly knows the importance of making people aware of what Our Lady requested at Fatima. He and his wife Dorothy have been good friends for a long time.

I also wish to thank all those at the Blue Army headquarters of the National Shrine of Our Lady of Fatima in Washington, New Jersey, who did the actual work of preparing the manuscript of this book for publication. I especially wish to acknowledge the important work of Vincent Covello who worked on reviewing and editing the material for the various chapters. Also I wish to acknowledge the great work for the layout, design and artwork done by Megan Pritchard. She put many hours into preparing a truly beautiful book.

Finally, I want to give a very special thanks to Bishop Frank Caggiano, the Bishop of the Diocese of Bridgeport, Connecticut. I only came to know the Bishop in the last couple of years. He has a very great love and personal devotion for Our Lady of Fatima. Despite his very busy and demanding schedule, he took time to write a beautiful foreword for this book. May Our Lord and Our Blessed Lady reward Bishop Caggiano for his kindness and generosity.

CHAPTER ONE

REFLECTIONS ON OUR LADY'S WORDS AT FATIMA
DEVOTION TO THE IMMACULATE HEART OF MARY

"Jesus wants to establish in the world
devotion to my Immaculate Heart."

Our Lady made her second appearance in the Cova da Iria in Fatima to Lucia Dos Santos [age 10], her cousin Francisco Marto [age 9], and his little sister Jacinta [age 7] on June 13th, 1917. It was a day of special religious celebration in Portugal. It was the feast of St. Anthony!

1

Because the word had spread after the first apparition of Our Lady on May 13th, 1917, a small crowd of about fifty people came to the Cova when they heard that "a beautiful Lady from heaven" would appear there on June 13th. When Our Lady appeared that day to the three little visionaries, Lucia, who acted as spokesperson for the three asked Our Lady: "What do you want of me?" Our Lady said that she wanted the children to return to the Cova on the 13th of each month up to the month of October and to pray the Rosary every day.

When Would the Children Go to Heaven?

Then Lucia raised the issue to Our Lady of when she would take the three of them to Heaven. (Our Lady had already told the children in her May apparition that she would take them all to heaven. Now Lucia wanted to know when that would be)! Our Lady answered that she would take Jacinta and Francisco to Heaven soon (and, in fact, they both died less than three years after the apparitions at the Cova ended). But for Lucia, God had other plans. Our Lady continued to speak: "Jesus wishes to make use of you to make me known and loved. He wants to establish in the world devotion to my Immaculate Heart."

Our Lady was very prophetic for Lucia. She remained on earth until she was 97 years old when she died as a Carmelite nun in Coimbra on February 13th, 2005. As the sole surviving visionary and witness to the Fatima message, Sister Lucia proved a faithful secretary and apostle of Our Lady, writing about the events of the apparitions in her memoirs.

Devotion to the Immaculate Heart of Mary
- It's Importance

Our Lady's words stress how important devotion to her Immaculate Heart is, since Jesus wants it established all over the world. At other times, Jesus spoke of this devotion. On one occasion, He said He wanted devotion to His Mother's Immaculate Heart joined to devotion to His own Sacred Heart! After all, devotion to Mary is a sure means of growing in love for Jesus. She never keeps us for herself; she always sends us to Him! This is clearly seen in her last recorded words in Sacred Scripture: "Do whatever he tells you!" (Jn 2:5).

Another example of Jesus' desire to share the importance of devotion to His Mother's Immaculate Heart occurred when Lucia, then a Sister of Saint Dorothy, was having so much difficulty getting Pope Pius XI to make a Consecration of Russia to the Immaculate Heart of Mary. Lucia asked Our Lord why He would not just grant the conversion of Russia without the consecration? Jesus answered that because of the consecration the whole world would know that the conversion of Russia and the promised era of peace would only come about through the intercession of His Mother's Immaculate Heart.

What Should Our Devotion Consist Of?

In our devotion to the Hearts of Jesus and Mary, the heart really stands for the whole person. Our devotion to the Sacred Heart of Jesus, then, really means our devotion to Jesus Himself as the Divine Son of God the Father, who also became the Son of Mary. We adore and thank Him for both His divine and human love in creating, redeeming, and sanctifying us. We honor and praise Him for all He did for us in His life, death, and resurrection.

When it comes to devotion to Our Lady, we focus on her total love for God and for us. This means we honor her for all she did in God's plan of salvation when she was on earth, and all she continues to do for us from Heaven. In honoring her great holiness, which many saints believed surpassed that of all the angels and saints, we honor God Himself who gave her such extraordinary graces. At the same time, we are moved to seek her constant maternal help and intercession, as well as imitate the virtues of her life. Let us look briefly at Mary's twofold role as part of the devotion to her Immaculate Heart.

Mary's Maternal Role: Mother of the Church

We best approach devotion to Mary's Immaculate Heart by beginning with her role in the plan of salvation. First and foremost, she became the Mother of God. God the Father had chosen her and prepared her to become the mother of His Divine Son by the Immaculate Conception. This gave her freedom from Original Sin and a fullness of grace. This was absolutely essential since Jesus was to take His very flesh and blood from her. At Nazareth, Mary's humble and obedient consent allowed God to become Man.

As St. Leo the Great put it: "The Son of God became the Son of Man, so that the sons of men might become the sons of God." At Bethlehem, she gave birth to the Son of God and Savior of the world. She presented Him for honor and veneration to the humble – to the shepherds, who in Venerable Archbishop Fulton J. Sheen's words "knew they knew very little," and to the Wise men, who in all their wisdom knew they did not know everything. Mary is now constantly presenting her Son to us, because she never wants to keep Him to herself.

Mary was again a mother at Calvary. On the cross Jesus was suffering for the Church to be borne mystically through the merits of His passion and death. That birth was seen in the truly sacramental sign of Blood (namely, representing the Eucharist, the greatest Sacrament of the Church) and Water (namely, representing Baptism, the Sacrament of entrance into the Church).

In addition, Our Lady was suffering below the cross. When she gave birth to Jesus at Bethlehem, she suffered no pain because neither she nor her Son had sinned. But as she was becoming the mother of Jesus' mystical Body on Calvary and we were all sinners, she suffered more than any other human could, except her Son, because she loved more than any other human could. "Woman, behold your Son!" These were sorrowful words received with love. "Behold your mother!" (Jn 19:26-27). These are words that should fill us with deep gratitude to Our Lady.

Finally, Mary was Mother of the Church at Pentecost. That was the birthday of the Church and, of course, the Mother of the Church had to be there. The Holy Spirit had overshadowed Mary at the moment of the Incarnation. Now, when the first disciples of Jesus who represented the Church were receiving the Holy Spirit, Our Lady would be there to teach us all how to respond to the Holy Spirit working in our lives. In our devotion to Mary's Immaculate Heart, we honor, praise and thank her for all these ways in which she promoted our salvation.

St. Augustine taught that Mary was not only Jesus' mother, but also His disciple. We usually do not think of her in that way. But St. Augustine insisted it was more important for Mary to be His disciple than to be His mother. That is because she like us had to grow in holiness by growing in the virtues – faith, hope, charity and all the rest. Mary has left us such great examples of the practice of virtues. If we are to be devoted to her Immaculate Heart, we have to imitate her virtues so as to be her true sons and daughters, and in this way grow in likeness to Jesus. We can only touch on some of these virtues briefly.

Her faith was seen in her belief in the message of the Archangel Gabriel. Once her question of how she could remain a virgin and yet become a mother at the same time was clarified by the Archangel, she did not hesitate to believe this was possible by God's grace, and so she gave her generous consent. Her humility was seen in her referring to herself as "the handmaid of the Lord" (Lk 1:38). She was always ready to serve and to do whatever the Lord wanted of her. Then her obedience was seen in her generous consent: "Let it be done unto me according to thy word" (Lk 1:38). She gave all praise to God for all she had received: "He who is mighty has done great things for me and holy is His Name" (Lk 1:49). We see Mary's prayerfulness by pondering in her heart God's word and all that happened to her. She was compassionate in her going in haste to assist her aged cousin, St. Elizabeth, at the Visitation.

At Cana we see her charity in wanting to save the newly-wedded couple from the embarrassment of running out of wine at their wedding reception. We see Mary's courage and steadfastness by accepting whatever sufferings God sent her as she stood as the mother of Sorrows at the foot of Jesus' cross. We see Mary's faithful love as she inspires all her children to do God's will as faithfully as we can with the help of His grace. When we consider all these things there can be no doubt why Jesus wanted devotion to the Immaculate Heart of His mother to be established throughout the world!

"Pray, Pray very much, and make sacrifices for sinners; for many souls go to hell, because there are none to sacrifice themselves and to pray for them."

This quote of Our Lady on August 19, 1917 is one that practically summarizes the entire message of Fatima, at least in terms of what she was asking of us! It is a call to prayer and penance, both of which are so essential to bringing about the conversion of sinners. As our heavenly Mother, Mary wants all her spiritual children to be saved by turning away from their sins, seeking God's forgiveness for them and amending their lives so as to live in a manner pleasing to God. This means to know God, to love Him and to serve Him in this world so that we might be happy with Him forever in Heaven. Once an individual has begun living a faithful Christian life to achieve their own personal salvation, Our Lady then asks them to join with her Divine Son Jesus in the all-important mission of saving the almost countless souls of others.

As we shall see, this can take many forms: sharing God's Word, good example, catechetical instruction, performing the corporal and spiritual works of mercy, spiritual direction and the like. Not everyone can do these things, but everyone with a sufficient understanding and practice of faith, hope and charity can actually do the two most primary works: namely, prayer and sacrifice! We are all called to do this for the salvation of souls!

Mary's Request Came During Her August Apparition

This apparition of Our Lady was the most unique of all six of them for a number of reasons. For one, Our Lady did not appear in the Cova da Iria as in her previous apparitions, but instead in a place called Valinhos located about a ten-minute walk from their village of Aljustrel. The little shepherds many times grazed their sheep there. The Angel of Peace made two of his three apparitions nearby, as well.

Another reason why this August apparition was unique was that it did not occur on the 13th of the month like the others, but rather on August 19th. The reason was that the three little visionaries, Lucia, Francisco and Jacinta, were secretly abducted by the then district administrator, Arturo de Oliveira Santos. He was a fallen-away Catholic, a leading

9

Freemason and a fiercely anti-clerical man. The reason he abducted the children was not only to prevent them from being in the Cova da Iria for their scheduled meeting with Our Lady, but also to torture and torment the little children by horrible threats of boiling them in oil if they did not reveal the secrets Our Lady had confided to them and then make a public statement that there really were no apparitions by Our Lady, but they had just made up the whole story. The children remained steadfast and would not give in! So Our Lady, having missed her appointment on the 13th, made it up to the children by appearing to them on August 19th.

Another difference in this apparition was that it was not "planned" in advance as to time and place. It happened quite suddenly. Lucia and Francisco were together with John, the brother of Francisco and Jacinta, at Valinhos grazing their families' sheep. When Lucia sensed the coming presence of the Blessed Mother and that she would appear at any moment, realizing that Jacinta might miss the apparition, she asked John to go and get his sister. He refused to do so until she "bribed" him with a few pennies for his efforts. As soon as Jacinta arrived, Our Lady appeared over a holmoak tree at the site.

Her visit was brief and her message simple. Our Lady told the children to continue to come to the Cova on the 13th, to pray the Rosary daily and that she would perform a miracle in October for all to believe in the truth of her apparitions. She also answered a question that Lucia put to her about what to do with money that people were leaving at the Cova. Our Lady told her to use some of it to make two litters (used to carry statues) for the coming feast of Our Lady of the Rosary (October 7th) and the rest was to be used to help construct a chapel that was to be built on the spot of the apparitions. Finally, Lucia asked Our Lady to cure some sick people. Our Lady responded that she would heal a number of them during the year, but added that it was necessary for some of them to reform their lives and return to God, while others needed to pray, especially the Rosary.

Our Lady's Plea for Prayer and Penance

Lucia tells us that suddenly, the face of Our Lady became sad. It was the sadness of a mother in mortal anguish over a horrible fate that threatened to come upon many of her beloved children! It was at that moment that Our Lady uttered her heartfelt plea of sorrow and anguish:

"Pray, pray very much, and make sacrifices for sinners; for many souls go to hell, because there are none to sacrifice themselves and to pray for them."

This plea of Our Lady brings us right into the heart of the redemptive mission of Christ. Jesus said that He had come that we might have life and have it more abundantly (Jn 10:10). We know that it is a central belief of our Catholic faith that Jesus gave His life to take away our sins by His death on the cross. He was the victimal Lamb offering Himself in sacrifice and in obedience to the Father's will. His Precious Blood was the price of our redemption. When He rose again on Easter Sunday, He destroyed the power of death and gave us the hope of eternal life. He has promised to raise all who love Him to eternal life on the last day. Theologians refer to what Jesus did for us in making Himself the offering or Victim for our sins as the "vicarious redemption." In other words, though we sinned He atoned for them. He suf-

11

fered in place of us and for us. But it is part of God's plan that others join Him in distributing the graces of Christ's redemption to all souls that they might be set free from Original Sin and personal sin, and that they might gain eternal life in Heaven.

Mary's Unique Share in the Redemption

No one shared more completely in Christ's redemptive mission than Our Blessed Lady. After all, Our Lord needed to be part of the human family if He was going to redeem all of humanity. So He needed a body and blood, as well as a human soul. He took His body and blood from the Virgin Mary when she gave her consent with such total generous abandonment to God's plan for the salvation of the world. She then shared in all His joys and sorrows from the moment of His conception to the moment of His death. Although it is not a defined dogma of the Faith, theologians and even Popes have referred to her role in God's plan as "Co-Redemptrix." This does not mean that she equally shared with Jesus in the work of redemption, for only Jesus could redeem us; but it does mean that she shared most intimately in the redemptive sufferings of her Son. The truly inspiring words of St. Bernard of Clairvaux express this so beautifully. It is found in the Divine Office for the Feast of Our Lady of Sorrows, September 15:

Do not be surprised, brothers, that Mary is said to be a martyr in spirit. Let him be surprised who does not remember the words of Paul, that one of the greatest crimes of the Gentiles was that they were without love. That was far from the heart of Mary; let it be far from her servants.

Perhaps someone will say: "Had she not known before that He would die?" Undoubtedly. "Did she not expect Him to rise again at once?" Surely. "And still she grieved over her crucified Son?" Intensely. Who are you and what is the source of your wisdom that you are more surprised at the compassion of Mary than at the passion of Mary's Son? For if He could die in body, could she not die with Him in spirit? He died in body through a love greater than anyone had ever known. She died in spirit through a love unlike any other since His.

Our Lady Reminds Us of Our Co-Redemptive Role

The plea that Our Lady made to the children for prayer and sacrifice was, in the final analysis, an invitation for them to share also in the redemptive mission of Jesus with her. The Lord wants us to do this. Very often in the Gospel we see people who shared in Jesus' mission of redemption. Some people brought certain individuals to Jesus to receive not only healing but forgiveness of their sins. This was true of the healing of the paralytic at Capernaum (cf. Mk 2:1-12), who was carried by his friends and placed before Jesus. Our Lord first forgave him his sins and then healed his paralysis. That paralytic could never have gotten to Jesus unless his friends carried him there. So in a spiritual sense, there are many people who never pray to God for the forgiveness of their sins. They may even be totally unaware that they are in danger of being lost from God for all eternity. Someone else will have to "carry them" by their prayers and sacrifices to Jesus. In other words, by the prayer and sacrifice Our Lady requested, we win the grace for sorrow for sins, conversion and forgiveness for those who are not asking for these graces for themselves. This can be especially seen in the "Pardon Prayer" taught to the children by the Angel.

"My God, I believe, I adore, I hope and I love You; and I beg pardon for those who do not believe, do not adore, do not hope, and do not love You!"

Our Lady's Sorrow at the Loss of Souls

After making her plea for prayer and penance, Our Lady adds the urgent reason why we must respond. She tells the three children and us, as well, that many souls go to hell because there is no one praying and sacrificing for them. The children, having already seen a vision of hell in the July apparition, know only too well how terrible that suffering was, and for all eternity! Remember, these sinners are not making reparation for their own sins, so Our Lady wants us to make reparation for them. There is no way that Our Lady could ever forget the immense suffering of Jesus on the cross precisely for the salvation of souls. So even for one soul to be lost, one of her own spiritual children no less, what sorrow this must cause her mother's heart. She heard the cry of Jesus on the cross, "I thirst." Not only was that thirst for physical drink, but His thirst was also a spiritual desire for the salvation of the whole world. He wanted none to be lost. So Mary's plea is an anguished cry that all may be saved and none may be lost. The way we can fulfill Our Lady's request is by our frequent prayers and sacrifices for sinners to be saved.

REFLECTIONS ON OUR LADY'S WORDS AT FATIMA
MARY'S PLEA FOR HOLINESS

"Our Lady Pleads with Her Children"

Much of Our Lady of Fatima's message deals with prayerful intercession for the conversion of sinners as well as reparation for the sins they have committed. Many such sinners are unfortunately in danger of being eternally lost from God. But Our Lady's final plea at Fatima goes even beyond that. She pleads for all of her children to stop sinning altogether. One can sense the deep sorrow in her heart at how our all Holy and Almighty God is offended so grievously and so frequently by the sins of His own creatures. Mary's sorrow is reflected in the remark Sister Lucia wrote when she described Our Lady as "looking very sad…!" Our Lady was seeking for all her children to lead good and holy lives which would be pleasing to Almighty God. Such holiness on the part of her faithful children would be a great source of reparation and honor to Almighty God who, as Our Lady said, has already been "so much offended."

The Horror of Sin

As no one else could possibly grasp the horror of sin, Our Lady surely knew it and experienced it in her anguish and suffering at the foot of the cross of Her Son. She knew in this sorrow that pierced her heart so profoundly what the real meaning of sin is. So many people today dismiss sin lightly as if it were simply a breaking of a law. So many laws change that people take a very casual attitude toward the binding effect of any law, even the law of God. Laws are meant to define true moral life. Jesus Himself in the Sermon on the Mount said He had come not to abolish the law or the commandments but to help us to understand how we can live it not only in our external actions but also with a proper disposition in our hearts. For example, He cited the Old Testament commandment, "You shall not kill" (cf. Mt 5:21), but He said if we even have hatred in our hearts toward our neighbor we would be guilty of murder in the heart. He said the same of the sixth commandment, "Thou shalt not commit adultery" (cf. Mt 5:27), because He said anyone who has the lust of adultery in their thoughts and desires has already committed adultery in the heart.

The suffering and death of her Son made Our Lady realize, as no one else could for no one could love Jesus as she did, how terrible and evil sin is. It created a debt to God that man could never pay by himself. If true reparation was to be offered to our Heavenly Father, then His Divine Son had to become man to save us for we could not save ourselves. The price was the suffering and death of Jesus seen in His Precious Blood that was shed for the

16

salvation of the world. The letter to the Hebrews (cf. Heb 12:24) tells us that the blood of Abel cried out to God for vengeance toward his murderer, his own brother Cain. In contrast, the blood of Christ cried out for mercy for sinners. We can say that Jesus renews this cry for mercy every time His Body and Blood are consecrated at the Holy Sacrifice of the Mass. In a sense, He repeats the cry for mercy that He uttered on the cross, "Father, forgive them, for they do not know what they are doing" (Lk 23:34). He offers His blood once again through the Mass to atone for our sins.

Sin in the Parable of the Prodigal Son

As we reflect on this beautiful parable (cf. Lk 15:11-32) of God's mercy, we gain insight into what sin truly is. First of all, the younger son demands from his father the share of the inheritance that was coming to him. How many people today take God's blessings for granted as if they were entitled to receive them. They forget His blessings are gifts freely given by God out of His good- ness and not that we have any right to them. When we sin, don't we also have the attitude "It's mine; I can do with it what I want." We forget that it was given to us as a gift by a loving God. The second thing we see in the parable is that the younger brother is ungrateful for what he has received because he just walks out on his father and his brother with no concern for their feelings or how his absence affects them. Sin always has the aspect of ingratitude to God. Finally, the young man began to live a very immoral life, giving himself over to the pleasures of the flesh. Ironically though, he could only do this be- cause he had the support of his father's money that he so boldly took with him. Isn't this at the heart of every sin: we use the very gifts of God to support us in our

17

sinfulness. Sin is a great betrayal of God's goodness. It was only when the money he had inherited ran out and, in a way, the bottom fell out of his life [The only job he could get was taking care of pigs and the Jewish people considered these animals unclean] that he came to his senses and realized he should go back to his father and ask his forgiveness.

We Need a Sense of Sin

Saint John Paul II said that our present society has lost a sense of sin. In other words, we do not look upon sin as a selfish offense against God's goodness and love. After all, God created us freely out of His love. At the same time He sustains us in our existence by His loving Divine Providence. Finally, He bestows His mercy and blessings generously upon us whenever we turn back to Him. Sin then becomes a terrible affront of ingratitude to a God who loves us so much.

We need to restore a sense of sin to our way of thinking. Years ago there was an expression, "It's as obvious as sin!" Today, we never hear that expression anymore. Sin has disappeared from people's minds and hearts; some consciences have grown lukewarm, others have grown cold. As a result, many people offend God and don't give it a second thought. People judge evils by how they affect them in their finances, in their pursuits of pleasure, in their sense of security and in many other worldly ways. How few stop to consider sin as offending the goodness of God. And we are merely His creatures!

Not all sins are equal in their offense to God. Many sins are sins of "weakness." We fail because human nature is easily disturbed by things which happen in
18

daily life. For example, we lose our patience easily, we make critical remarks, dilly-dally with temptations that should be quickly and decisively expelled. It is important that we recognize these sins and express our sorrow to God for them. Other sins are sins of "ignorance." This means we commit them because we lack a knowledge of what we are really doing or the offense to God involved in them. Sometimes people fall into habits such as cursing or making snap-judgments. In many of these instances people are not aware that they are offending God. We should not excuse these sins, but we should be sorry for them even though we commit them out of weakness or ignorance.

But the sins we have to work on the most are those of "malice." These are the sins of which we are aware when we are committing them but still deliberately do them. This would be knowingly blaspheming God's name, or looking at pornography which fills one with a spirit of lust, or deliberately lying to make ourselves appear better, or having a prideful attitude of disdain for others. These latter sins are more offensive to God. If we are going to heed Our Lady's plea to stop offending the Lord our God, we must start with the deliberate sins of malice in our life.

How Can We Restore a Sense of Sin in Our Lives?

Jesus said in the Gospel that because sin would become so widespread in later times, the faith of many will grow cold (cf. Mt 24:12). One step we can take to restore a personal sense of sin in our lives is to correct any false sense of entitlement that would make us look at our freedom and our blessings in life as things that I have every right to as if God owes it to me. We have to realize that God's blessings and our freedom are His gifts and must be used in the way He wants us to use them, for His honor and glory, and for our salvation and eternal happiness. Another consideration that would help with this is to have some sense of the fear of God. When the bad thief on Calvary turned to Jesus, he did so with an attitude of mocking Christ saying, "Are you the Messiah? Save yourself and us!" (Lk 23:39). He was only thinking of his own earthly happiness. We then read how the good thief, Dismas, responded:

The other [thief], however, rebuking him, said in reply, "Have you no fear of God, for you are subject to the same condemnation? And indeed, we have been condemned justly, for the sentence we received corresponds to our crimes, but this man has done nothing criminal." Then he said, "Jesus, remember me when you come into your kingdom." He replied to him, "Amen, I say to you, today you will be with me in Paradise" (Lk 23:40-43).

The good thief had a sense of sin insofar as he recognized that he had to give God an accounting of his life. In this realization, he saw his own responsibility for his sins. He trusted Jesus enough to ask for forgiveness. That was the difference between one thief being saved and the other being lost.

A final and very necessary help to avoiding sin is to cultivate the frequent practice of Confession. Most Catholics do not seriously examine their consciences until they are preparing for Confession. If we do not have a sense of our sinfulness, how can we work to overcome our sins? We need to be aware of our sins and then to be motivated to remove them from our lives. This is the fruit of contrition in which we express our sorrow for our sins because they have offended God, Who is deserving of all our love as well as offending our neighbor and even ourselves. Part of contrition includes amending our lives. We form a resolution to overcome our sins by practicing the opposite virtues. In this way, our lives will become holy, and we will eliminate or at least lessen our offenses against God and His goodness.

Our Lady Will Help Us

One of the things Our Lady's coming to Fatima reminds us of is her great concern for our salvation and sanctification. She was given her vocation as Mother of the Church on Calvary: "Woman, behold your Son" (Jn 19:26). She fulfilled her role in her last years on earth for the first generation of the disciples of Jesus. But even after her Assumption into Heaven, she continues her motherly role. She pleads for us for mercy from her Son. She intercedes for us for the graces to grow in holiness, and she is always ready to receive us, even in our most sinful moments. Do we not call her the "Refuge of Sinners?" Then let us not forget how many times, when we pray the Hail Mary, we invoke her saying "Holy Mary, Mother of God, pray for us sinners now and at the hour of our death." If we make sincere efforts to avoid sin in our lives and stop offending God, we can be very confident that Mary will be interceding for us in our final moment on earth to lead us to Heaven.

"In the End, My Immaculate Heart will Triumph. The Holy Father will Consecrate Russia to Me, and She will be Converted, and a Period of Peace will be Granted to the World" (July 13, 1917).

The apparition of Our Lady at the Cova da Iria on July 13, 1917 contains the most important part of her message for the salvation of souls and the peace of the world. From this one apparition we learn of the "three secrets"

22

of the Fatima message. The first secret dealt with the children seeing a vision of hell. Our Lady did not allow them to see this to scare them. She had already told them they were going to Heaven. What she wanted was that the children would testify to the very existence of hell so as to warn all her spiritual children to live good Christian lives so that they would not end up in eternal damnation.

The second secret of July 13th dealt with Our Lady's words about the end of World War I and the possibility of another more terrible war which unfortunately was World War II. She then added her reference to the rise of communism in Russia that would spread around the world provoking wars, famine, annihilation of nations, persecution of the Church and the Holy Father. We will return to Our Lady's reference to communism and how she would ultimately be victorious over it.

The third secret was finally revealed by Saint John Paul II on May 13, 2000 during the Mass he celebrated in the Cova da Iria for the beatification of Francisco Marto and his sister Jacinta. Both Sister Lucia and Cardinal Ratzinger, now Pope Emeritus Benedict XVI, assured us that the full third secret has been revealed and there is nothing more hidden about the message of Fatima. Much could be said in proof of the full disclosure of the third secret, but our focus in this reflection will deal with the promised triumph of the Immaculate Heart of Mary.

An Evil Will Begin in Russia

As stated briefly above, Our Lady foretold to the children the rise of the evil of communism in Russia. However, she immediately added a message of hope:

"I shall come to ask for the consecration of Russia to my Immaculate Heart and the Communion of Reparation on the First Saturdays. If my requests are heeded, Russia will be converted, and there will be peace; if not, she will spread her errors throughout the world, causing wars and persecutions of the Church. The good will be martyred, the Holy Father will have much to suffer, various nations will be annihilated."

Anyone familiar with world history knows how accurately Our Lady predicted the future. Since the end of World War II, the United States has been involved in two major wars to prevent the spread of communism, namely in Korea and Vietnam. Many countries under communist domination suffered starvation by famines that were deliberately brought about by Russia such as in the Ukraine where millions of people were starved to death under communist tyranny. The Church found herself persecuted in many countries under communist domination such as in Eastern Europe. There is still great persecution of Christians in China, Vietnam, and North Korea. All of this Our Lady foretold. The Popes, beginning with Pius XI and even continuing with Saint John Paul II and Pope Emeritus Benedict XVI, have suffered various forms of persecution which bear a communist influence.

But Our Lady Also Gave a Word of Hope

Although the evils Our Lady foretold would be brought about ultimately by Russian communism, she left us with a great promise of hope. She said that this evil would not have the ultimate victory. Rather she would bring about the lasting victory.

"In the end, my Immaculate Heart will triumph. The Holy Father will consecrate Russia to me. She will be converted, and a period of peace will be granted to the world."

These words are extremely important for they attest to something Our Lady said would actually happen. It is a factual, declarative statement. (Russia will be converted!) It is not qualified by the word "maybe" or "perhaps"; it is simply declared as a fact that will happen and no doubt Our Lady was not uncertain, confused, or ambiguous. According to Our Lady's words, the consecration had to occur.

There have unfortunately been voices saying that the consecration that Saint John Paul II did on March 25th, 1984 with nearly 3,000 bishops was not valid. Approximately 800 bishops were actually right in the Vatican that day joining the Holy Father in the consecration prayer. The remaining bishops were carrying out the consecration in union with the Holy Father in their various archdioceses and dioceses throughout the world.

Did the Holy Father In Union With the Bishops of the world correctly consecrate Russia to the Immaculate Heart of Mary?

The words of Our Lady in her July apparition, namely, "the Holy Father will consecrate Russia to me" stated as we have seen a fact that would undeniably happen. Otherwise, we must conclude that Our Lady does not have the power to bring about the consecration or that Jesus would not do this for her as her words said would happen. This would be preposterous to believe. There-

fore, the consecration has to be made to fulfill Our Lady's statement. Now various objections have been made,
casting some doubt over whether the consecration was
ever properly made. One thing that we should absolutely
keep in mind is the fact that the consecration properly
carried out by Saint John Paul II with the bishops of the
world happened while Sister Lucia dos Santos was alive.
When asked if the consecration was valid, Sister Lucia
said "Heaven accepted it." She later on restated her position that the consecration had been carried out by Saint
John Paul II with the bishops of the world. Now, if the
consecration was not validly carried out and Sister Lucia
dos Santos is no longer with us, who would possibly be
able to declare the consecration valid? Many people say
the Pope did not do it properly. These people certainly
would not accept that the Pope, as the one able to declare
it, validly carried it out. So who would declare that it was
validly carried out? I can't think of anybody that people
would accept to do this if the Pope, the very Vicar of
Christ on earth is not trusted. That would mean we would
then have to conclude that Our Lady's words are wrong,
namely, that the Pope cannot consecrate Russia to her
Immaculate Heart. In my opinion, this would border on
blasphemy against Our Blessed Lady.

Let's Look At
What the Real Problem Is

Many people have said to me that if the consecration
was properly carried out by the Pope in union with the
bishops of the world, then there would be peace in the
world. Yet, in fact, we have very serious threats of war
and violence in many places of the world, even the possibility of a nuclear war catastrophe. A woman recently said to this author: "If the consecration was made

properly, then Our Lady said world peace would occur immediately!" But Our Lady did not say that. That is a mistaken assumption. Remember, Our Lady said she would come and ask for two things to prevent the spread of communism. One was the consecration of Russia to her Immaculate Heart by the Pope with the bishops of the world. That was done by Saint John Paul II and the bishops of the world, and Sister Lucia confirmed that it was done. But Our Lady asked for a second thing which she called the "Communion of Reparation" or the Five First Saturdays Devotion.

This is the part of the request of Our Lady that has not been responded to adequately. In fact, Sister Lucia used to say that the Five First Saturdays Devotion is the most neglected part of the Fatima message. After all, Our Lady's request at Fatima was for our prayers, sacrifices, sufferings, and the living of good Christian lives as the means to achieve the salvation of souls. The peace of the world would then follow. This is the part we must do so that we can assist in the full carrying out of Our Lady's request.

Changes Are Occurring in Russia

Most people are not aware of the great changes that are taking place in Russia since the consecration occurred. Remember, suffering for 75 years under a ruthless, atheistic rule which systematically tried to destroy all signs of God, the Russian people have had to rebuild their faith. Since the consecration took place, some startling facts have occurred. In 1989, only five years after the consecration, the terrible Berlin wall that separated East from West was taken down by the people who put it up without a shot being fired! Who would have ever thought that possible? In 1991, on Christmas Day, the flag of the Soviet Union came down over the Kremlin and the flag of Russia, a free Russia, went up in its place. Mikhail Gorbachev, then the President of the Soviet Union, declared on that day that the Soviet Union was ended.

Between 1985, the year after the consecration and 2011, the number of churches in Russia has increased by 350%. From 1991 to 2011, the number of monasteries in Russia has increased from 117 to 802. That is an enormous increase, especially when you consider the tremendous loss of Religious in the Christian West in that same period. Our Lady's words are being fulfilled. Her triumph will happen, even soon, if we all do our part in living good Christian lives, praying the Rosary daily, offering our sacrifices for the conversion of sinners and carrying out the Five First Saturdays Devotion which is directed toward overcoming atheism in Russia and the secularism that communism has spread around the world including the United States of America. Mary's promise is our greatest hope during these difficult times. Let us heed Our Mother's call from Fatima!

CHAPTER TWO

THE SEERS OF FATIMA
JESUS AND MARY CHOOSE
THE HUMBLE AND CHILDLIKE

At the Last Supper, Jesus said to His Apostles: "It was not you who chose Me, it was I who chose you to go forth and bear fruit!" (John 15:16). It is always God who chooses those to whom He will give His gifts. For example, those who are Catholic have been called to the gift of faith and Baptism, so that now, we dare to pray: "Our Father, who art in Heaven..." God further calls us to our personal vocations within the Church, the Priesthood, Consecrated Life, Married Life and Single Life in the world. Perhaps most unique among God's calls, however, is His choice of those who would have a special mission among His people or be entrusted to spread a special message among them. We may now ask the question: what does God base His choices on? Can we point to a common quality in those He chooses?

The Choice of King David

The choice of King David shows us that God does not base His choices on external appearances or qualifications, which we humans usually do, but upon what is in the heart. After King Saul had been rejected by God for his disobedience, God directed the prophet Samuel to go to Bethlehem and anoint one of the sons of Jesse as the new future king of Israel:

As [the sons of Jesse] came, Samuel looked at Eliab and thought, "Surely the Lord's anointed is here before Him." But the Lord said to Samuel: "Do not judge from his appearance or from his lofty stature, because I have rejected him. Not as man sees does God see, because man sees the appearance but the Lord looks into the heart" (1 Sm 16:6-7).

After all these sons of Jesse were presented to Samuel, and he was not directed by God to anoint any one of them as king, Samuel asked Jesse:

"Are these all the sons you have?" Jesse replied, "There is still the youngest, who is tending the sheep." Samuel said to Jesse, "Send for him…" Jesse sent and had the young man brought to them. He was ruddy, a youth handsome to behold and making a splendid appearance. The Lord said, "There—anoint him, for this is he! Then Samuel, with the horn of oil in hand, anointed him in the midst of his brothers; and from that day on, the spirit of the Lord rushed upon David…" (Ibid. 16:11-13).

King David was considered too young and basically not mature enough to be considered a possible future king. Yet, God chose him, and he served the Lord (despite a fall in weakness) so faithfully that God called him "a man after my own heart!"

St. Paul Describes Those God Chooses

In writing his first letter to the Corinthians, St. Paul gives a very honest description of those whom God calls:

"Brothers, you are among those called. Consider your own situation. Not many of you are wise, as many account wisdom; not many are influential; and surely not many are well-born. God chose those whom the world considers absurd to shame the wise; He singled out the weak of this world to shame the strong; He chose the world's lowborn and despised, those who count for nothing, to reduce to nothing those who are something, so that mankind can do no boasting before God" (1 Cor 1:26-29).

This is not a very flattering description. It shows that God, as they would say in the sports-world, does not usually choose "the first-round draft choices," that is, the most promising and talented. In fact, we might actually say that He picks individuals who are "least likely to succeed." As (Mother) St. Teresa of Calcutta would say, "God does not choose the qualified, but He qualifies those whom He chooses."

Shepherds and Wise Men

One more example is helpful. Who found their way to the manger at Bethlehem at the birth of Jesus? Ven. Archbishop Fulton Sheen used to say that there were two groups of people who came to see the Infant Jesus, shepherds and wise men. Ven. Archbishop Sheen stressed that both groups were humble. He said the shepherds knew they knew very little, and so came to find the "Infant Good Shepherd." The Wise Men knew that in all their wisdom, they did not know everything, and so they followed the star that led them to the new-born King of the Jews, the very King of Kings. Only the humble of heart could accept belief in a God who became man, and the King of Heaven who became poor for our own sake, wrapped in swaddling clothes and lying in a manger!

Why does God Choose
the Humble and Childlike?

Let us look briefly at two reasons. First, the humble and childlike have a simple openness to truth, to all truth, not to just some or only ones they agree with. With a childlike trust, they readily accept what they perceive as true, especially as revealing something to them. The proud, the arrogant and the sophisticated, on the other hand, often put up barriers against what they do not want to believe. All kinds of objections— usually deep-seated prejudices—arise in their minds and hearts. Some of these are intellectual: "I know better than that!" Some are emotional: "I would never feel right about accepting that idea!" And some are simply threatening to them, consciously or unconsciously: "If I believed that, I'd have to change my whole lifestyle." Archbishop Sheen used to say that the easiest thing to prove is the existence of God, but it is the hardest thing to accept! Why? Because if I admit there is a God who made the universe, then I am not my own "god," and so I cannot do whatever I want to! This is why many secular scientists have rejected from the scientific community any other scientist who appeals to the argument of "Intellectual Design"—a

Creator Who made the order in the universe, which is so obvious that I can know what time the sun will rise tomorrow! "Political correctness" is undermining morality, science, and even common sense!

A second reason why God chooses the humble and childlike is because their simple belief and conviction will motivate them to be more courageous in carrying out the mission confided to them. Many of those whom God chose for special missions in His plan often encountered stiff opposition—disbelief, threats, persecution, violence and even death. They needed an unwavering trust to carry them through these challenges. Once the childlike believe, they can be very firm in their conviction! As someone said, "One person with a belief is equal in force to 99 who merely have an interest."

Examples of the Humble and Childlike

In the Gospel, Jesus praised His Heavenly Father, saying, "Father, Lord of Heaven and earth, to You I offer praise; for what You have hidden from the learned and the clever You have revealed to the merest children! Father, it is true. You have graciously willed it so!" (Mt 11:25-26). Throughout history, God has not changed His ways. In fact, we must all become childlike! "Let the little children come to Me. Do not shut them off. The reign of God belongs to such as these. Trust Me when I tell you that whoever does not accept the kingdom of God as a child will not enter into it" (Lk 18:16-17). This is clearly seen in many of the apparitions of Our Lady, particularly at Fatima (which we will see in depth in following articles). Here, let us look at some other Marian visionaries, and we will see that they were truly humble and child-like, if not always actually children. We can only reflect on a couple of brief examples.

Our Lady of Guadalupe
and St. Juan Diego

The Blessed Virgin Mary appeared to a 57 year old widower, an Aztec Indian named Juan Diego. She appeared four times to him from December 10 to 12, 1531. He was a truly childlike and humble man, and the conversations between him and Our Lady reflect this. Juan Diego was going to a special Marian Mass when Our Lady appeared to him on Tepeyac Hill, then a few miles outside Mexico City, and addressed him affectionately, "Juanito, Juan Dieguito!" The name "Juan" is John in Spanish. But the little suffix "ito" added at the end of the name is a diminutive, and is usually used in addressing children. We might translate this endearing term as "Little Johnny". Then Our Lady called him, "Juan Dieguito". The name "Diego" is James in Spanish. This might be rendered, "John! Little Jimmy!" She was addressing him affectionately as a little child. He, in turn, with childlike simplicity, addressed Mary as "My Lady, my Queen and my little Girl". There is no doubt this exchange of address to one another demonstrates that this conversation is one between a loving Mother and her childlike son!

When Juan Diego went to Bishop Zumárraga to present Our Lady's request of him to build a chapel on Tepeyac Hill, he was not believed, for the bishop needed proof in order to be convinced. When he returned to Our Lady and she asked how things went, he replied:

"My dear little Mistress, Lady, and Queen, my littlest
34

Daughter, my dear little Girl, I went where you sent me to carry out your order...The way he answered me I could clearly see that he thinks I may have made it up... So I beg you, my Lady, Queen and my little Girl, to send one of the nobles who are held in esteem and respected with the message, so that it will be believed; for I am a man of no importance...a follower."

The Blessed Mother responded:

"Listen to me, my youngest and dearest son, know for sure that I do not lack servants and messengers to whom I can give the task of carrying out my words, who will carry out my will. But it is very necessary that you plead my cause and, with your help and through your mediation, that my will be fulfilled."

It should be noted that Our Lady's words calling Juan Diego "my dearest, littlest, and youngest son" could also be understood as "my humblest and most child-like" of sons.

Our Lady of Lourdes and St. Bernadette

Our Lady appeared to a poor peasant girl named Bernadette Subirous in the remote town of Lourdes, France from February 11, 1858 to July 16, 1858. Bernadette was a simple, illiterate girl with frail health, but she was very humble and childlike. Bernadette was so simple that she often did not understand what Our Lady was telling her. When Bernadette asked for her name, Our Lady said, "I am the Immaculate Conception." Bernadette dutifully reported this to the parish priest, but admitted that she had no idea what it meant.

On another occasion when Our Lady urged Bernadette, "Pray! Pray the Rosary for the conversion of sinners," Bernadette was not afraid to ask as a child, "What does that mean?" Knowing she would not understand, Our Lady merely answered her, "Pray the Rosary."

Bernadette also had the zeal of a child. She did not hesitate to go into the grotto where Our Lady appeared, even though it was a garbage dump visited only by pigs, and she did not stop going even when the whole town mocked her and the police threatened to imprison her. Bernadette also described herself without airs. Many challenged her claim to have seen Our Lady, but Bernadette answered, "Don't I realize who I am? Our Lady chose me because I was the most ignorant. If she could have found anyone more ignorant, she would have chosen her." Bernadette understood how much Our Lady loves the humble and childlike, so when the Church authorities asked her: "Why would the Mother of God appear to a 14 year old girl", she simply answered, "I guess she wanted one."

THE SEERS OF FATIMA
LUCIA DOS SANTOS

She Received a Special Mission
from Our Lady

[As we know, God often chooses "little ones" to reveal great messages to the world.]

Of the three little shepherd children that Our Lady appeared to at Fatima, Lucia dos Santos and her two cousins, Francisco Marto and his little sister Jacinta, Lucia was the oldest. She was just ten when Our Lady appeared to them in 1917, while Francisco was nine and Jacinta only seven. Since she was the natural leader of this little band of three, she became the spokesperson and was the only one who actually spoke to Our Lady. She was to outlive her younger cousins by many years, fulfilling a special mission Our Lady gave her to spread the urgent message of Fatima and devotion to Her Immaculate Heart throughout the world.

Early Childhood Background

Lucia was born on March 22, 1907, in her family's home in a little hamlet called Aljustrel, one of a number of small hamlets which made up the parish of Fatima. She was baptized a few days later in her parish church. Lucia was the daughter of Antonio and Maria Rosa dos Santos. She was the youngest of seven children, six girls and one boy. Being the youngest, she was the "favorite," and so she received a great deal of affection from her family. God provided that Lucia, as well as Francisco and Jacinta, would be born into deeply religious families, where they were taught the Catholic Faith, an ardent love of God, living the Commandments and daily prayer, especially the Rosary. Antonio took care of the family farm, raising crops and caring for the livestock. Maria Rosa cared for the family's needs in the home. She was generous in helping the poor and the sick, while also teaching catechism classes to some of the young children in the parish. The Santos' were an exemplary Christian family.

First Confession and
First Holy Communion

For many Catholic children, First Confession and First Holy Communion produce beautiful lasting memories of Jesus' mercy and love. This certainly happened with Lucia. To begin with she received these Sacraments when she was only six years old, at a time when the Church required children to be at least seven years of age.

Lucia, who had already received some of her instructions from her mother at home, was sent by her mother to accompany some of her siblings who were taking instructions from the parish priest in preparation to receive the Sacraments. Often in class the parish priest would call on little Lucia to answer questions that some of the older children could not answer. However, when it came time to receive Confession and Holy Communion, the parish priest said Lucia could not because she lacked the required age. However, a visiting priest who examined her on how well she knew Church teaching on the Sacraments was so impressed that he intervened on Lucia's behalf and obtained the parish priest's permission for her to receive the Sacraments.

Here is a special grace Lucia received at her First Confession:

"After listening to me, the good priest said these few words: 'My child, your soul is the temple of the Holy Spirit. Keep it always pure, so that He will be able to carry on His divine action in it.' On hearing these words, I felt myself filled with respect for my interior, and asked the kind confessor what I ought to do. 'Kneel down there before Our Lady and ask her with great confidence, to take care of your heart, to prepare it to receive her beloved Son worthily tomorrow, and to keep it for Him alone.' In the Church, there was more than one statue of Our Lady; but as my sisters took care of the altar of Our Lady of the Rosary, I usually went there to pray. That is why I went there on this occasion also, to ask her with all the ardor of my soul, to keep my poor heart for God alone. As I repeated this humble prayer over and over again, with my eyes fixed on the statue, it seemed to me that she smiled and, with a loving look and kindly gesture, assured me that she would. My heart was overflowing with joy, and I could scarcely utter a single word" (Fatima in Lucia's Own Words, pp. 55-56).

Lucia's First Holy Communion also held many special graces for her. The night before, her sisters had made her a beautiful white dress and a wreath of flowers. Lucia was so excited to be receiving Our Lord the next morning and even try on her white dress, that she could hardly sleep the whole night. In the morning she got up and put on her special dress. Then a very simple but meaningful ceremony happened. Lucia described it this way: "Then my sister Maria took me into the kitchen to ask pardon of my parents, to kiss their hands and ask their blessing." This ceremony reminds us of Our Lord's words: "If you bring your gift to the altar and there recall that your brother has anything against you, leave your gift at the altar, go first to be reconciled with your brother, and then come and offer your gift" (Mt 5:23-24).

Lucia was not so much offering a gift at the altar that day as receiving the Gift of all gifts, the Body, Blood, Soul and Divinity of Jesus Christ. No doubt her act of humility, reverence and love for her parents made her soul that much more pleasing to the Lord when He came to her. Lucia described what happened next:

"My mother gave me her last recommendations. She told me what she wanted me to ask Our Lord when I had received Him into my heart, and [she] said goodbye to me in these words: 'Above all, ask Him to make you a saint.' Her words made such an indelible impression on my heart that they were the very first that I said to Our Lord when I received Him. Even today, I seem to hear the echo of my mother's voice repeating these words to me….As soon as I arrived at the church, I ran to kneel before the altar of Our Lady to renew my petition. There I remained in contemplation of Our Lady's smile of the previous day" (Fatima in Lucia's Own Words" p.56).

Here is what Lucia tells us about that glorious moment of her First Holy Communion:

"The parish priest came down and passed among the rows of children, distributing the Bread of Angels. I had the good fortune to be the first one to receive. As the priest was coming down the altar steps, I felt as though my heart would leap from my breast. But he had no sooner placed the Divine Host on my tongue than I felt an unalterable serenity and peace. I felt myself bathed in such a supernatural atmosphere that the presence of our dear Lord became as clearly perceptible to me as if I had seen and heard Him with my bodily senses. I then addressed my prayer to Him: 'O Lord, make me a saint. Keep my heart always pure for You alone.' Then it seemed to me that in the depths of my heart, our dear Lord distinctly spoke these words to me: 'The grace granted to you this day will remain living in your soul, producing fruits of eternal life.' I felt as though transformed in God."

Lucia and the Apparitions of the
Angel of Peace and of Our Lady

These extraordinary graces which Lucia received when she was only six would serve as a solid foundation for her future mission in God's plan. First there came in 1916 three apparitions by an angel who called himself, "the Angel of Peace." He taught the children many important things, like praying and sacrificing for the conversion of sinners as well as the importance of making reparation to Jesus in the Eucharist for the "outrages, sacrileges and indifference" He receives from so many.

The angel was preparing them for a special mission of prayer and suffering they would be asked to carry out for the peace of the world. Lucia was nine at the time, while Francisco was eight and Jacinta only six. Lucia was the only one of the three to speak with the angel. As a result of the angel's teachings, the children grew to have a generous spirit of sacrifice, prayer and concern for the salvation of souls. These would be very necessary for the mission that lay ahead of them.

In the following year of 1917, Our Lady of Fatima appeared six times to the three visionaries. In her first apparition on May 13th Lucia asked if the three shepherds would go to Heaven, and Our Lady said yes. Then Our Lady put a very serious question to these little ones: "Are you willing to offer yourselves to God and bear all the sufferings He wills to send you , as an act of reparation for the sins by which He is offended and of supplication for the conversion of sinners?" With great enthusiasm, the children responded immediately, "Yes. we are willing." And they did suffer, especially Lucia. Her own family, particularly her mother, did not believe about Our

Lady's apparitions. Lucia was ridiculed by neighbors, questioned by both civil and ecclesiastical authorities, and even threatened by the Masonic district governor with death by being boiled in oil.

Without doubt, one of Lucia's most difficult sufferings came during Our Lady's second apparition on June 13th. Lucia asked Our Lady if she would take the children to Heaven. Our Lady's response was: "Yes, I will take Jacinta and Francisco soon. But you are to stay here some time longer. Jesus wishes to make use of you to make me known and loved. He wants to establish in the world devotion to my Immaculate Heart." This must have been a great sorrow for Lucia. She longed to go to Heaven, but now she would have to wait. [She died at age 97!] She would also be separated from her cousins, whom she loved as the friends of her childhood. She then asked Our Lady if she would be alone after her cousins went to Heaven. Our Lady assured her: "No, my daughter. Are you suffering a great deal? Don't lose heart. I will never forsake you. My Immaculate Heart will be your refuge and the way that will lead you to God."

Lucia lived nearly eighty-seven more years from the time God entrusted this mission to her. All through those many years, she remained faithful to the task of spreading devotion to the Immaculate Heart of Mary. Now she is very happy with Jesus and Mary and her cousins in Heaven forever!

The Seers of Fatima
Blessed Jacinta Marto

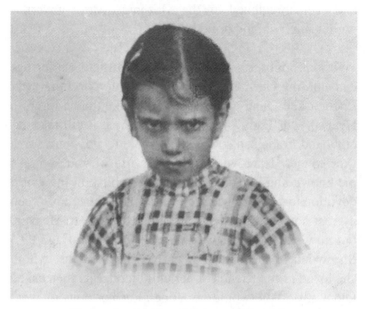

Young in Age but Mature in Sanctity

People may wonder why God would have ever chosen a six year old girl to be one of three shepherd children who would receive a message of immense importance for the salvation and peace of the world. But when we see how generously Blessed Jacinta Marto responded to Our Lady's message, we immediately realize the wisdom of God's choice. Sometimes children are surprisingly responsive to God's love, and to the requests He makes of them. This was surely the case with little Jacinta.

Family Background

Jacinta Marto was born in the little village of Aljustrel in the parish of Fatima in Portugal on March 11, 1910. She received Baptism on March 19th. Her parents were

Manuel Pedro Marto and Olympia de Jesus dos Santos. They were also parents of her brother Francisco. Jacinta was the seventh and youngest child in the family. Her parents were very devout Christians who gave their children a solid religious and moral education. Jacinta likewise attended catechism lessons given by her maternal aunt, Maria Rosa dos Santos, the mother of Lucia.

From her earliest age Jacinta showed a deep piety, which included a love for prayer and the truths of her faith as well as proper care in the choice of her friends. She had a very lively and joyful disposition, and loved to play, especially to dance. Her brother, Francisco, was always ready to play her a tune to dance with on his little flute. However, her personality had some glaring defects. She had a strong inclination to dominate in choice of games and the like. She also disliked being contradicted, so much so that she easily pouted when she didn't get her way. Finally, she was possessive of what she won at games and was reluctant to return her winnings to their rightful owners. Sister Lucia, in her first memoir, gives us a frank description of her little cousin Jacinta:

"Before the happenings of 1917, apart from the ties of relationship that united us, no other particular affection led me to prefer the companionship of Jacinta and Francisco to that of any other child. On the contrary, I sometimes found Jacinta's company quite disagreeable, on account of her oversensitive temperament."

"The slightest quarrel which arose among the children when at play was enough to send her pouting into a corner…even the coaxing and caressing the children know so well on how to give on such occasions, were still not enough to bring her back to play; she herself had to be allowed to choose the game, and her partner as well. Her heart, however, was well-disposed. God had endowed her with a sweet and gentle character which made her at once loveable and attractive. I don't know why, but Jacinta and her brother Francisco had a special liking for me and almost always came in search of me when they wanted to play. They did not enjoy the company of the other children, and they used to ask me to go with them to the well at the bottom of the garden belonging to my parents …. Not a few times, I found myself unable to do what my little friend wanted" (Fatima in Lucia's Own Words, Postulation Center, Fatima, Portugal, 1976 pp 20-22).

This description makes a person think of one of (Mother) St. Teresa's favorite sayings: "God does not choose the qualified, but He qualifies those whom He chooses." Heartfelt prayer and a generous spirit of sacrifice changed Jacinta completely.

Some Characteristics of Jacinta's Devotion

Jacinta loved to contemplate Christ crucified and when she listened to her mother tell stories of His Passion, she wept. Lucia described an incident of Jacinta kissing Christ on a crucifix: She kissed it and hugged it with such devotion that I have never forgotten it. Then, looking attentively at the figure of Our Lord, she asked: "Why is Our Lord nailed to a cross like that?" "Because He died for us." "Tell me how it happened," she said (pp 23-24).

As a result, she was resolved never to sin because she did not want Jesus to suffer any more.

Another characteristic of Jacinta was her love of nature.

She loved to watch beautiful sunsets and contemplate the stars in the sky. The children called the stars "Angels' Lamps." The moon was "Our Lady's Lamp" and the sun was "Our Lord's Lamp." She said that she liked Our Lady's Lamp better because it doesn't burn up the children or blind them the way Our Lord's Lamp does.

One of the most striking characteristics of Jacinta's spirituality was her very generous spirit of sacrifice for the conversion of sinners. It started with the three apparitions of the Angel of Peace in 1916. The Angel taught the children to offer prayers and sacrifices for the conversion of sinners. Little Jacinta, therefore, became quite generous in offering sacrifices such as giving away the nice lunch her mother had made for her to poor children and in turn eating very bitter herbs and nuts. She would even forego drinking water on hot days as a sacrifice. The Angel Prayer sums up this spirit: "My God, I believe, I adore, I hope and I love you! I beg pardon for those who do not believe, do not adore, do not hope and do not love you." The children recited this prayer frequently with the desire to bring souls to God. But what really intensified Jacinta's spirit of sacrifice was her seeing the vision of hell during Our Lady's apparition to the three visionaries on July 13th, 1917.

After the vision, Our Lady told the children they had seen hell where poor sinners go and that God wanted to prevent this by establishing devotion to Mary's Immaculate Heart in the world. Lucia wrote that the vision of hell profoundly affected all three of the visionaries, but Jacinta, the youngest, seemed to be especially moved. Every penance and mortification was nothing in her eyes if it could only prevent souls from going there. She often recited the prayer Our Lady taught them at that time: "Oh

47

my Jesus, forgive us our sins, save us from the fires of hell and lead all souls to Heaven, especially those most in need of thy mercy."

Another aspect of her intense prayer life was her special love for the Holy Father. Jacinta was privileged to have two visions of the Holy Father. In one of them, she saw the Pope suffering deeply.

"I saw the Holy Father in a very big house, kneeling by a table, with his head buried in his hands, and he was weeping. Outside the house, there were many people. Some of them were throwing stones, others were cursing and using bad language. Poor Holy Father, we must pray very much for him" (Memoirs p106).

Our Lady in her July apparition had foretold the spread of Communism with the results that the Church would be persecuted and, as a consequence, the Holy Father would have much to suffer.

Jacinta Went Quickly to Heaven

After the apparitions ended with the great miracle of the sun on October 13th, 1917, Francisco and Jacinta were taken to Heaven within three years. Francisco died on April 4th, 1919 while Jacinta died February 20th, 1920. Jacinta had become very generous in her willingness to suffer for the love of the hearts of Jesus and Mary, and for the salvation of souls. She would be even more heroic as her death approached.

Jacinta told Lucia that Our Lady appeared to her and Francisco and told her that she would take Francisco to Heaven soon. Then Our Lady asked Jacinta if she wanted to come to Heaven around the time Francisco would come or if she wanted to stay on earth longer to suffer for the conversion of sinners. When Jacinta said that she wanted to stay for the salvation of souls, Our Lady told her that she would be suffering much. Jacinta went to two different hospitals as Our Lady had foretold, but as she said it was not to be cured, but to suffer for the love of God and the conversion of sinners and in reparation for the offenses committed against the Immaculate Heart of Mary.

There she suffered tremendously from frequent fevers, from an abscess on her side, pneumonia, and tuberculosis. Hardest of all was that she suffered all alone, without family or friends. Just before Our Lady came to take her to Heaven, she appeared to Jacinta and told her that her sufferings and sacrifices saved 50,000 souls.

While in a hospital in Lisbon, Our Lady appeared to Jacinta and told her several things of great importance. Here are some of the things Our Lady revealed:

- That war is a punishment for sin.

- That many fashions would come that would offend Our Lord very much.

- That many marriages are not of God.

- That priests must be very pure and concentrate on their mission to the Church and souls, and be obedient to the Pope and their Superiors.

- That more souls go to hell because of sins of impurity than for any other.

Little Jacinta died in Lisbon. She was first buried in a cemetery in Ourém. Later, her body was moved to the parish cemetery of St. Anthony in Fatima and buried near her brother Francisco. Later she was placed in a side chapel in the Basilica at the Fatima shrine.

Both Jacinta and Francisco were beatified by Saint John Paul II on May 13th, 2000. We hope that someday soon they will be canonized.

THE SEERS OF FATIMA
BLESSED FRANCISCO MARTO

A Shy Boy Blossoms with Holiness

When Our Lady chose Francisco, she must have had a big smile on her face. If his little sister Jacinta had to overcome her tendency to get the things she wanted by controlling others and pouting if she didn't get her way, young Francisco had to overcome a tremendous shyness and a tendency to be indifferent about a lot of things. In the end, he became very dedicated and although still a bit shy, he exemplified a real courage to do all that Jesus and Our Lady asked of him. God's grace made a marvelous change in this young boy. As this is written, he is now blessed and may well be declared a saint soon.

Family Background

The parents of young Francisco Marto were Pedro "Ti" Marto and Olympia de Jesus. He was born in the little village of Aljustrel on June 11, 1908 and was baptized on June 20th. His parents were modest farmers and good Christians. Young Francisco was a sincere, obedient, kind and diligent young boy. He received a very sound education from his parents, as well as from the catechism classes he attended, which were taught by the parish priest and his aunt, Maria dos Santos, the mother of Lucia. The beginning of his faith and love for God, and his desire to pray occurred in the home. But it extended beyond that because he participated in the religious activities of the parish. He was always friendly and smiling, especially helping those neighbors who were in need and showing great compassion for sick people. He was a calm and peaceful child and at ease with adults as well as with children of his own age. He had no difficulty adjusting to others even if they irritated or contradicted him. He had a great love of nature and delighted in seeing the mountains, and the rising and setting of the sun. Like his sister, Jacinta, he called the sun "Our Lord's Lamp" and was filled with joy at the appearance of the stars which he named the "Angels' Lamps."

He was so simple in his innocence that he said when he got to heaven he would have to put oil in the lamp of the Virgin Mary (the moon).

At about the age of six, Francisco began to take care of the flock of sheep that belonged to his family. Beginning early in the morning he would daily lead them out to pasture and in the nice weather would not return until sunset. He took with himself his lunch and his flute with which he amused himself. Many times he was accompanied by his sister Jacinta. One of the things he liked to do was play the flute for his sister, Jacinta, who in turn liked to dance. They made a perfect match! They would join their cousin, Lucia, who was pasturing the family's flock.

The Angel Apparitions

In the spring of 1916 the three little shepherds received the first vision of an angel who called himself the "Angel of Peace" or the "Angel of Portugal." This spiritual wonder made little Francisco become more generous in sacrifices for the salvation of souls and more intense in prayer. He frequently recited the prayer the angel taught the children to offer for the salvation of those who did not believe, or adore, or hope, or love. After the angel apparitions, he often tended to be alone to think and pray in solitude. He would hide behind rocks and trees while at other times he would climb to the highest and most solitary places so that he could meditate and pray without distractions from others.

After the angel brought the children the Eucharist during his third apparition to them, young Francisco felt a very ardent and almost constant longing to be near Jesus (Whom he called the Hidden Jesus) in the Blessed Sacrament, although he was only permitted to receive Holy Communion shortly before he died.

Despite his great virtues, Francisco did have a few shortcomings. One of them was an attitude of indifference, which Lucia felt was his greatest defect. For example, if someone took something belonging to him, he would simply shrug off the injustice and say: "Let him have it!

53

What do I care?" At other times he could be a bit mischievous. For example, he loved animals. He played with lizards and snakes, often bringing them home where they were quite unwelcome. However, he was especially fond of birds and always saved some of his bread so he could feed them crumbs.

Our Lady Appears

The apparitions of Our Lady of Fatima, beginning on May 13, 1917, made a great impression on all the children. Young Francisco experienced a deepening of the flame of God's love in his heart and his desire for the salvation of souls. His one goal was to pray and suffer according to Our Lady's request. He lived the message of Our Lady's call to holiness with great joy and fervor and constancy, and proclaimed it by prayer and penance. He used to say, "How beautiful God is, how beautiful! But He is sad because of the sins of men. I want to console Him, I want to suffer for love of Him."

When the three children were threatened by the governor of Ourém to boil them in oil if they did not make a statement that the apparitions were not true (that they made up the whole idea), and that they would reveal the secret that Our Lady told them to keep, it was young Francisco who strengthened his cousin Lucia and his sister Jacinta not to be afraid. Every time the local authorities threatened him with death, he would reply, "If they kill us, we will soon be in heaven! Nothing else matters!"

After Our Lady's Apparitions Ended

Francisco, within two years after the apparitions ended, contracted influenza in the terrible epidemic that took about 20 million lives all over the world. As he had become generous in his sacrifices, he was now courageous in his suffering. In his final illness he desired to make reparations for sinners through his suffering. He began to experience flu symptoms on the way to school one day, but he preferred praying in church to returning home. He told Lucia, "I have such a bad headache and I feel as though I'm going to fall." She said, "Then don't come. Stay at home!" He answered, "I don't want to. I'd rather stay in the church with the Hidden Jesus while you go to school" (Lucia's Memoirs, p. 141).

Another example of his suffering is described by Lucia in one of her memoirs: "While he was ill, Francisco always appeared joyful and content. I asked him sometimes: 'Are you suffering a lot, Francisco?' He answered, 'Quite a lot, but never mind, I am suffering to console Our Lord and afterwards, within a short time, I am going to heaven!'" (Lucia's Memoirs p. 143).

Like saints who reach a high degree of sanctity, Francisco arrived at such an ardent desire for heaven that he no longer found any interest in the things of earth. After all, Our Lady had promised he would go to heaven soon after the apparitions. Here is an interesting dialogue between Francisco and some ladies who questioned him about what he wanted to be when he grew up:

"Do you want to be a carpenter?"
"No, madam."
"A soldier?"
"No, madam."
"Surely you would like to be a doctor?"
"No, not that either."

"Then I know what you would like to be…a priest! Then you could say Mass and preach…"

"No, madam, I don't want to be a priest either."

"Well, then, what do you want to be?"

"I don't want to be anything. I want to die and go to heaven…"

Francisco's father, who was listening to this conversation, told the women that heaven was his son's heart's desire (From The Beginning, p. 171 as quoted in Fatima Today, p. 136).

Yes, Francisco died on April 4th, 1919. Before he did so, he asked pardon from his family for all his faults. Then little Jacinta, with tears in her eyes, said to her brother, "Give my love to Our Lord and Our Lady and tell them I'll suffer as much as they want, to convert sinners and to make up to the Immaculate Heart of Mary." At 10 o'clock in the morning, Francisco said to his mother, "Mother, look at that lovely light by the door!" It was the sign Our Lady was coming to take her little Francisco to heaven. Now he would be forever with "his beautiful Lady."

After his funeral Mass, his body was buried in the parish cemetery of St. Anthony's Church in Fatima. On March 12th, 1952, his remains were transferred to a side chapel in the Basilica built at the site of the Cova da Iria. He was beatified with his sister Jacinta on May 13th, 2000 at Our Lady's shrine at Fatima by Saint John Paul II.

CHAPTER THREE

THE MESSAGE OF FATIMA: FATIMA IS A CALL TO LIVE BY FAITH

Living by Faith

I chose as a common theme for this series to write on the message of Fatima and how it calls us to live by Faith. What I hope will be evident throughout this series is that if we live the message that Our Lady gave us at Fatima, our personal faith will grow much stronger. At the same time, it will have an increased effect on the very life and mission of the Church, which is the Mystical Body of Christ.

Already Called to the New Evangelization

In 2010, Pope Benedict XVI issued an apostolic letter establishing a "Pontifical Council for promoting the New Evangelization." He explained that a spiritual darkness has come over many traditional Catholic countries, especially in Western Europe and North America. This has hindered people in the growth of their faith, and has left many incapable of distinguishing between good and evil. He said that the New Evangelization had to be directed, not simply at those who have not yet heard of Christ and His Church, but primarily at those who once had believed and were once active members of the Church but now have abandoned their faith and moral living. Here is how Pope Benedict put it in the Apostolic Letter:

"In the course of history, this mission [namely, 'the duty of the Church to proclaim always and everywhere the Gospel of Jesus Christ'] has taken on new forms and employed new strategies according to different places, situations and historical periods. In our own time, it has been particularly challenged by an abandonment of the faith, a phenomenon progressively more manifest in societies and cultures which for centuries seemed to be permeated by the Gospel. The social changes we have witnessed in recent decades have a long and complex history, and they have profoundly altered our way of looking at the world....This has not been without consequences on the religious dimension of human life...There has been a troubling loss of the sense of the sacred which has even called into question foundations once deemed unshakable such as faith in a provident Creator, God, the revelation of Jesus Christ as the one Savior and a common understanding of basic human experiences: i.e., birth, death, life in a family, and reference to a natural moral law."

Saint John Paul II
and the New Evangelization

One of the greatest tasks of the long papal reign of Saint John Paul II was to lead the Catholic Church into the Third Millennium. As part of his preparation for the Jubilee Year 2000 he expressed a deep sense of the need for a New Evangelization:

"I sense that the moment has come to commit all the Church's energies to a new evangelization ... no believer in Christ, no institution of the Church, can avoid this supreme duty: to proclaim Christ to all peoples!"

He also added that the Holy Spirit is the principal agent of the New Evangelization. For this reason, then, the Church must constantly invoke the Holy Spirit on all of her communities and ministries.

Faith: The Foundation of
the Christian Life

The Council of Trent taught that faith is the beginning, the foundation, and the measure of the Christian life. In other words, we begin to live our Christian life based on our belief that God exists, and that He created us and called us to a new life with Him through Baptism. This new life reaches its fulfillment when we are called to eternal life with God in Heaven. Then, faith will give way to the glorious vision of God for all eternity. St. Paul said of faith that we see now obscurely as in a darkened mirror, but in Heaven through the beatific vision we will see God clearly as He is (cf. 1 Cor 13:12). It is absolutely important, however, to remember the Apostle's other words that while we are here on earth, the just person must live by faith and not by sight (2 Cor 5:7).

60

Secularism, the Modern
Enemy of Faith

Our faith rests in the conviction that God is real, that He calls each one of us to eternal life. What has entered into our society in a most insidious way is even now seeking to enter the Church by a growing sense of secularism. In fact, Ven. Archbishop Fulton Sheen said that secularism, the spirit of the world that removes God from all aspects of society, is the greatest challenge to the Catholic Church in our time. Let us for a moment briefly compare how the Christian person and the secular person view life. The Christian view of life is that we were created by God to live in this present world as a time of test of our love for Him. If we are found worthy by our faithfulness and through His mercy that forgives us our sins, Christians hope to enter the Kingdom of Heaven.

The secular person looks on life quite differently. In the true secularist view of life, there is no afterlife. This life is all there is, and so "what you see is what you get." This is why secularists live for all the pleasures and satisfactions that this world can give because for them there is no belief or hope in a life beyond. As one secular phrase would have it, "Eat dessert first!" This is not a new idea! St. Paul, when writing about the resurrection of the dead in his first letter to the Corinthians stated that there were many who did not believe in the Resurrection. These people also lived for this life only. He quoted the popular pagan slogan of the day: "Eat, drink, and be merry for tomorrow we die!" (1 Cor 15:32).

Our Lady's Message Counters
the Secularism of Our Time

What Our Lady spoke of to the three little children of Fatima, Lucia, Francisco, and Jacinta, was a message that emphasizes that Heaven is real. It also makes it clear that our supreme responsibility is to live in such a way in this world that we may be found worthy to come to the Kingdom of Heaven. She also warned us that the alternative would be to lose our souls in Hell forever! Mary's message, then, clearly sets before us a choice of life or death, of eternal bliss or eternal misery. She came with compassionate love to warn her children that they must live good Christian lives. She was deeply concerned that all her children would be saved and none would be lost. She expressed this again with great sorrow when she told the children in her August apparition: "Pray, pray very much and make sacrifices for sinners; for many souls go to hell, because there are none to sacrifice themselves and to pray for them."

The Faith of Many Will Grow Cold

One of the most unsettling statements of Our Lord in the Gospel is when He said that in the end times, because sin will be so widespread, the faith and love of many will grow cold. This author often wonders if we are coming to this critical state. So many people today seem to have less faith in God, less desire to live in a way that pleases Him, and less concern to arrive at the Kingdom. The most obvious cause of this terrible state is the widespread darkness of sin and immorality, especially sexual sins! When abortion, which is the legalized murdering of innocent human life, is accepted in a society, this is a sign of great decadence.

When same-sex marriage is being upheld as the equivalent of marriage as God gave us between one man and one woman, we are immersed in a moral decline. Unless we reverse these directions by re-establishing the sanctity of all life from conception to natural death and unless we uphold the sanctity of marriage between one man and one woman and not same-sex unions, the moral reform we need for faith to thrive once again would be impossible. This is why heeding Our Lady's call at Fatima and living as she asked us to is absolutely essential to living by faith once again. Sin, especially serious sin, undermines the life and vitality of faith.

Renewing Our Faith

How can we renew and reinvigorate our faith especially in such a very secularized society such as our own? Let me offer four ways that we can strengthen faith. First of all, we must live faithfully by God's commandments. This entails, above all, avoiding sins which offend our Creator and Savior. As Our Lady told the children in her October 1917 apparition with a heartfelt plea: "Do not offend the Lord our God anymore because He is already so much offended." Jesus said that by keeping His commandments we show Him that we love Him. Such faithfulness in choosing God and His demands above our own selfish pursuits is a sign we are living by faith. We may not see God, but we are choosing to love Him and to serve Him above all else!

A second way to strengthen faith is obviously to receive the sacraments regularly. The beautiful Sacrament of Confession has been neglected by many of our Catholic people today. Our Lady, no doubt, wanted to encourage her children to receive this important sacrament of peace and reconciliation with God when she asked as part of the Five First Saturdays Devotion that her children go to Confession once a month. If we neglect this sacrament, we will not experience the stirring of our faith through the profound peace that fills our souls after we have made a good Confession. How many people today live daily lives burdened with guilt, shame, and fear that could easily be removed by the Sacrament of God's mercy and peace? It may be difficult at times to tell our sins in Confession to a priest for we all have a certain sense of shame for the wrongs we have done. But how does that compare with the peace and joy that usually flood our souls when we bring our sins before the priest in the confessional? As Christ's representative, he absolves us from our sins. He unties us or sets us free from the burden of our guilt and shame, allowing the peace of Christ to abundantly enter our hearts.

A third thing we must do to restore our faith is to perform works of charity and mercy. Today our society is characterized by a great sense of narcissism or self-centeredness. This preoccupation with one's self results in excluding from our minds and hearts the true needs and concerns of others. We need to break from this self-focus by a spirit of sacrifice and doing good for others. The three little visionaries learned to make sacrifices for the conversion of sinners. Some of the sacrifices they made were to give their tasty homemade lunches to children far poorer than themselves and to be satisfied with eating wild berries and bitter nuts. They learned to share by denying themselves. This is something we need to return to in our own practice of the faith. As we deny ourselves the goods and pleasures of the body, the blessings and joys of the Spirit will be renewed within us.

A final way to invigorate our faith, and perhaps the point at which we must begin the process, is to pray. Someone once said that what water is to a fish, prayer must be to a Christian: we can't live in any other environment! Some years ago there was a phrase that was going around from a secularist philosopher by the name of Frederick Nietzsche; namely, "God is dead!" One of the best rebuttals to Nietzsche's claim was on a car bumper sticker: "My God is alive and well; I just spoke to Him this morning!" At Fatima prayer played a very important role. For example, when the Angel of Peace appeared to the children in 1916 he taught them two prayers. One was a prayer to ask pardon for those who did not believe, adore, hope in and love God. The other was the Prayer of Reparation to Jesus in the Most Blessed Sacrament for the many "outrages, sacrileges and indifferences" by which His enemies dishonor Him in His Eucharistic Presence.

Our Lady herself encouraged the children to pray the Rosary every day. When we ourselves pray the Rosary we are being formed in the methods of prayer beginning with vocal prayer [the prayers we recite like the Our Father and Hail Mary], then mental prayer [when we meditate in our minds on the Mysteries of the Rosary], and finally affective prayer [the prayers that spontaneously spring from our hearts in our own words]. These three forms of prayer are usually referred to as "The Prayer of the Lips; The Prayer of the Mind; and The Prayer of the Heart." Most of us probably learned our prayers from our mothers, fathers, and grandparents. Mary was just a good mother teaching all her children how to pray through her Rosary.

If we follow these four ways, we will be living by faith and doing what our Heavenly Mother at Fatima asked us to do for the salvation of souls and the ultimate peace of the world.

THE MESSAGE OF FATIMA:
FATIMA IS A CALL TO LIVE BY FAITH
THE FATIMA MESSAGE STRESSES
MANY IMPORTANT CHURCH TEACHINGS

Faith serves as the very foundation of the new life we receive in Christ through Baptism. This is because we cannot see God, but yet we still believe He exists, that He loves us and is calling us to share eternal life with Him in the Kingdom of Heaven. We also do not see many of the realities that we believe occur in our Christian life, but because Christ has revealed them to us, we place our trust in His Word and therefore we believe. For example, no one has ever seen Jesus present in the Eucharist; yet after a priest consecrates the bread and wine with the words Jesus said at the Last Supper, we believe it is now the very Body and Blood, Soul and Divinity of Jesus Christ. Another example would be that we cannot see sin being removed from the soul of someone receiving absolution in the Sacrament of Penance; yet we believe that those sins are forgiven. Although we do not rely on this fact, many people experience a sense of great peace after they have received absolution. But it is our faith that tells us that the sins are forgiven for those who confess sincerely and with a good intention to reform their lives. All of this adds up to the reason the Letter to the Hebrews states: "The just person lives by faith" (10:38). Furthermore, we read in the same letter "Without faith it is impossible to please (God), for anyone who approaches God must believe that He exists and that He rewards those who seek Him" (Heb 11:6).

Faith Has a Twofold Effect

Faith affects us in two ways. First it affects our minds by helping us to believe and then gradually understand the truths that God has revealed. These truths serve as the foundation of the way we live our lives, the beliefs that guide us. Second, faith affects our hearts by moving us to have confidence to believe in God, His working in our life and His providential care to lead us to eternal salvation. This is the daily living out of our faith. Though we do not see God, we believe He is always with us, providing for us and protecting us. By faith we trust that everything He does works to His honor and glory as well as our salvation.

Faith Gives Truth
to the Mind

Sacred Scripture, along with Sacred Tradition, provide us with the revelation God has made over the centuries to His people. This revelation began in Old Testament times but was completed by the public revelation of Jesus' teachings to His people who formed His Church and ended officially with the death of the last Apostle. Since they were revealed, these sacred truths have been preserved, proclaimed and even expounded by the Magisterium or teaching authority of the Church, namely, the Pope and the Bishops who are the official successors of St. Peter and the Apostles. It was to these latter that Jesus gave the commission to go throughout the whole world, even to the very ends of the earth, to proclaim the Gospel message to all men and women. This public Magisterium or teaching authority is assisted in its task of proclaiming and expounding on these revealed truths by the work of theologians and scholars who study the truths of our Church, delving deeper into their meaning and importance. The Magisterium's teaching, as well as the scholarly insights of those who support the Magisterium, help us to understand these truths more fully and clearly. This is called the "development of dogma."

After the official public revelation of the Church ended with the death of the last Apostle, no new dogma can be added to the "deposit of faith." (This expression refers to the complete summation of all the truths God has revealed in and through His Church.) So, if someone claims that an archangel appeared and said that there are now two new sacraments, we would have to reject this teaching as false because it would contradict the Church's official teaching that there are seven sacraments and no more. However, as we said, new insights and clearer understandings are gained through the proper development of dogma.

The Role of
Private Revelation

We may ask at this point, where do "private revelations" fit into the proper development of dogma? The official "public revelation of the Church" gave us the "full deposit of faith" which the Catholic faithful must accept, believe in and live by because they were revealed by God who can neither deceive nor be deceived. Any other revelations are considered "private revelations." It does not depend on how many people received that revelation. For example, an estimated 75,000 people saw the "Miracle of the Sun" at Fatima. But it is still considered a private revelation because it was not contained in the official revelation of Jesus and the Apostles.

All Catholics would be obliged to believe the truths contained in the "public revelation" as the Church teaches them in her Magisterium. However, Catholics are not obliged to believe in other teachings or messages contained in "private revelation." For example, Catholics are not obliged to believe in the private revelations of St. Faustina about the Divine Mercy message, or believe the messages revealed to St. Bernadette at Lourdes. That being said, we must add that it would be quite foolish not to believe in these messages because the Church has thoroughly studied these apparitions and declared them authentic.

Fatima is a private revelation, but one that has certainly been approved by the Church. Private revelations then do not add any new teachings (dogmas) to the Church's official teaching but they usually emphasize certain teachings that are important in the current life of the Church. Fatima, for example, reminded us of our co-redemptive mission to cooperate with the Lord and even with His Blessed Mother in the work of the salvation of souls. Likewise, Our Lady warned us of certain evils that would come upon the world, especially Communism, and how we can through prayer and penance halt the spread of these evils.

Fatima Emphasizes Certain Church Dogmas

Fatima touches on many official truths of our Catholic faith. In fact, Fatima has often been called a "compendium of the faith" which means it contains many Church doctrines. We can see that many of these Church teachings needed to be stressed again in the lives of Catholics today, since many of these teachings have been questioned or even denied in recent years.

Purgatory Is Real

One of the doctrines that people often dismiss as unimportant or even nonexistent is the teaching on Purgatory. The existence of Purgatory is an official teaching of the Catholic Church and therefore should not be denied. Many non-Catholic Christians deny the existence of Purgatory because they reject the Old Testament books of Maccabees, which clearly illustrate the need to pray for the dead, which assumes a place of temporary purification, before entrance into Heaven. Some Catholics have adopted that same thinking, which means that Purgatory is either denied or dismissed as unimportant. When most people die, their souls are not entirely free from sin or attachment to sin. If a person dies with mortal sin they will be sent to hell. But if they die with venial sins on their soul, they need a place of purification before entering into the presence of the absolute holiness of God

Himself. This is why Purgatory exists. The Catechism of the Catholic Church defines Purgatory in this way:

A state of final purification after death and before entrance into Heaven for those who die in God's friendship, but were only imperfectly purified; a final cleansing of human imperfection before one is able to enter the joy of Heaven (cf. III Purgatory 1030).

At Fatima the question of Purgatory came up in the very first apparition of Our Lady. During the course of the conversation with Our Lady, Lucia asked if two young women who were friends of one of her sisters and who had recently died were already in Heaven. The first one was Maria das Neves who died at the age of sixteen. Our Lady said that she was already in Heaven. She must have led a very good life to be so ready to go so quickly to Heaven. When Lucia asked about the second friend, Amélia, Our Lady responded with a remark that must have shocked the children: "She will be in Purgatory until the end of the world." One can only wonder what the state of her soul was like at the moment she died that her purification would take so long.

These references to Purgatory should remind us to lead good and holy lives. Even though the souls in Purgatory have the great consolation of knowing that when their purification is over they will go immediately to Heaven, still their suffering there is intense. It is far better to live a holy life so that we might spend as little time as necessary in this place of purification. St. Thérèse actually believed that if we daily fulfill God's will faithfully, we can even bypass Purgatory completely. I always think to myself "I'd like to take the non-stop flight to Heaven when God calls me!"

Hell Is Real

Hell is not an easy topic to think, write, or talk about. We know that God did not make hell for human beings. Rather it was created to punish the devil and his fallen angels. But if we die with unrepentant mortal sin we can no longer gain the gift of sanctifying grace necessary to enter the Kingdom of Heaven.

Many people today continue to live seriously sinful lives, because they accept the self-illusion that hell does not exist. People say a good and merciful God would never send anybody there. The problem is, those who do not repent of their sins send themselves to hell for they choose to hold on to their offenses against God rather than repent of them. Therefore we must be careful of the illusion that we can live any way we want, even a life of great immorality, and God will still save us. People simply want to block the idea of hell out of their minds and hearts. But this is precisely why Our Lady let the children see hell, so that they might warn people. Little Jacinta, who was only seven, used to say: "I wish everybody would see the vision of hell, and then nobody would go there." Our Lady wanted the children to be her messengers to motivate us to live good lives as well as to pray for those who are in jeopardy of going to hell. It was right after the children saw the vision of hell that Our Lady taught them the prayer we recite after every decade of the Rosary: "Oh my Jesus forgive us our sins, save us from the fires of hell. Lead all souls to Heaven especially those most in need of thy mercy."

Confession Is Necessary

A final teaching of the Church that was stressed at Fatima was the need for regular monthly Confession. Because of the weakness caused by Original Sin and our own personal sins and attachment to evil, we all experience temptations and even daily falls into sin. These sins burden us down in many ways. Before it is forgiven, sin causes us to feel a sadness of heart, as well as a sense of being distant from God. That is why when we confess our sins properly and with true sorrow and the purpose of amendment of our lives, the priest who forgives us says: "I absolve you from your sins in the name of the Father and of the Son and of the Holy Spirit." Most people do not realize that the word "absolve" comes from the Latin which means "to untie someone from a burden." That is precisely what Confession does. It sets us free from the burden of sin to love God, our neighbor, and even ourselves properly. It brings the healing presence of God's peace and mercy.

When Our Lady came to ask for what she called the "Communion of Reparation," (or "the Five First Saturdays Devotion"), she listed four steps necessary to practice on five consecutive first Saturdays. The first of these four elements was Confession. What it amounts to, is that Our Lady wants her children to go to Confession at least once a month. This will keep the conscience of her children close to God. Today when the faith of so many people seems weak, the need for Confession is even greater than ever. We are surrounded by so many temptations and enticements to do evil. God's mercy sets us free. This is why Our Lady stressed this beautiful sacrament given by Jesus through His Church. Our Lady wants her children to be authentically holy. So let us not neglect this sacrament in our personal lives so that we may experience the profound peace that comes when we hear those beautiful words, "And I absolve you from your sins ..."

Faith Gives Trust in the Heart

In addition to faith giving us truth in the mind by believing the things God has revealed and taught to us through the Catholic Church, faith also stirs up trust in our hearts. This faith in our hearts obviously rests upon the belief of truth in our minds. In other words, we believe the wonderful things God has revealed to us primarily through Christ, His Divine Son, and through the Church He founded. Then we can truly have a confident trust in God's providential care for us because He has revealed to us His unspeakable love and mercy. In other words, what truth is to the mind, trust is to the heart. Everything God has done for us from creating us, redeeming us, granting us His graces and promising us the Kingdom of Heaven if we are faithful, all inspire and urge us to

75

trust Him completely. The letter to the Hebrews (11:1) says, "faith is confident assurance concerning what we hope for." Because of what we believe about the Lord, we place ourselves completely into His hands to care for us. This we call God's "Divine Providence." One of the most beautiful things I have ever heard expressed about God's providence was from Fr. Lacordaire, O.P: "All I know about tomorrow is that God's providence will rise before the sun." In other words God is always preparing things for our good. He guides us in His ways so that we may carry out His will, live in His love, and come to the rewards He has promised us. He brings about good even in our times of uncertainty and difficulty. We might say that God's providence is like a compass that always tends toward the north. God uses all things for His honor and glory as well as for our salvation. They are simply two sides of the same coin.

Someone expressed this trusting aspect of faith in a beautiful acronym. Taking each letter of the word faith they described faith as a "Fantastic Adventure In Trusting Him." We all need to have great trust in God, and what we believe must reassure us that He wants us to have this trust. Without doubt we will be tested in our trust in Him, but we can be sure that He wants us to have the confidence of a little loving child in a loving father or mother. Faith has a very childlike quality to it. The Hebrew sense of this trust was that of little children secure in the arms of their parents.

Trust Overcomes Our Fears

Fear is the enemy of trust. Our fears prevent us from giving ourselves completely to God. They make us hesitant and prompt us to hold back. Many people are afraid to put their trust in God because they do not know what would lie in store for them if they did. Someone once said that "control is the name of the game." We like to feel that we are in control of the events of our life. We are afraid to give that control to anyone else, even God. Sometimes we question and fear that we are not good enough to allow God to work through us. We think He may just abandon us because He is not pleased with us.

Fear Takes Many Forms

There are many fears that affect us. There is the fear of the unknown when we find ourselves in uncertain circumstances. There is the fear of not being in control, as when we believe that situations are far beyond any remedy. There is also the fear that God may demand too much of us. And finally, there is the fear of those dark moments in our life when God seems far away. But Jesus encourages us to have great trust in Him especially in our trials. Sometimes they are trials of sickness, financial worries, marital struggles, lack of faith and practice of religion by members of our families, and spiritual darkness. But in all of these things Christ can and has conquered. If we trust in His power and love to help us, we will experience what Jesus called "the faith to move mountains" (cf. Mk 11:22-23). Loving trust moves God's power to work and nothing can resist that.

Where This Trusting Faith Was Lacking

Despite the fact that Our Lord had divine power, He would not use it unless there was a trusting faith in Him. Our Lord, on a few occasions, before granting a healing; e.g. for blindness or leprosy, He asked those who wanted Him to heal them: "Do you believe I can do this for you?" When they answered in the affirmative, He would sometimes say "Let it be done to you as you have believed" (Mt 9:28-29). On the other hand, where faith was lacking, He often could not work any miracles. The Gospel tells us that Jesus could work only a few healings in His hometown of Nazareth because their lack of faith distressed Him so much.

Where This Trusting Faith Was Weak

There were instances when Jesus was with His own Apostles that He pointed out to them their weakness in faith. One of the most striking examples was when Our Lord was in a boat with His Apostles in the Sea of Galilee and a terrible storm arose. We read in one account of this incident: "A violent squall came up. The waves were breaking over the boat so that it was already filling up. Jesus was in the stern, asleep on a cushion. They woke him and said to him, 'Teacher, do you not care that we are perishing?' He woke up, rebuked the wind, and said to the sea, 'Quiet! Be still!' The wind ceased and there was great calm. Then He asked them, 'Why are you terrified? Do you not yet have faith?' They were filled with great awe and said to one another: 'Who, then is this whom even the wind and sea obey?'" (Mk 4:37-41).

On other occasions, Jesus challenged those with little faith to have greater trust in His work. One very significant incident was that of the royal offical from Capernaum. This offical approached Our Lord who was in Cana of Galilee to come to his home in Capernaum, which was an approximately ten hour walk away. He asked Jesus to "come down and heal his son who was near death." Jesus said to him: "Unless you people see signs and wonders, you will not believe." The official's faith was so weak that he would only be reassured Jesus could help him if he could actually see Jesus touch his son and heal him that way. But Our Lord in turn challenged the man to trust His word and go home and his son would be better. The gospel tells us, "The man believed what Jesus said to him and left." He found his son healed because he believed in Jesus' word (Jn 4:46-54).

Where This Trusting Faith Was Fervent

Even when Our Lord found great faith, He often would challenge it so that it would grow even greater. This He did in various incidents in the Gospel. For example, when a group of Jewish leaders came to Jesus on behalf of a pagan Roman centurion who asked Jesus to heal his servant, Jesus immediately began to journey toward the centurion's home. But when the Roman officer realized that Jesus was coming, he felt that he was not worthy to have Jesus enter his home. Perhaps he was very conscious that the Pharisees would not enter the homes of pagans. So he did not want to place Our Lord in a position of entering a Gentile's house. But unlike the royal official above who would only be sure that Jesus would heal if He only touched his son, this Roman officer did not have to see that to believe. He knew that Jesus had authority to heal just as he, as a Roman centurion, had authority over a hundred soldiers. All he needed to do was to give an order to one of his soldiers "Go!" And he knew the soldier would carry out the mission he was given. Or he could send word to another soldier "Come!" And he knew that soldier would make his way to him. He did not have to see in order to believe. So he sent word to Our Lord in the beautiful words that we echo just before receiving Our Lord in Communion at every Mass: "Lord I am not worthy that you should enter under my roof! But

79

only say the word and my servant will be healed!" (Lk 7:1-10). Our Lord's response was unmistakable. "Amen! I say to you, I have not found such great faith in all of Israel!" And the servant was healed from that moment.

Our Lady Encourages Trust at Fatima

We might say that the whole message of Fatima is great encouragement to trust in God's presence and working both in our personal lives as well as in the life of the Church and in the world as a whole.

Trust in the Power of Prayer

Perhaps the most central part of our response to Our Lady's message was the call to prayer in a more ardent and confident way. Our Lady foresaw the evils that would come upon the world later on in the Twentieth Century, like a second world war, atomic bombs and the spread of atheistic Communism and the persecution of the Church. What she requested most were prayers for God's intervention to bring peace to a world torn apart by war and violence. Our Lady had told the youngest visionary, Jacinta, that war was a punishment for sin. She had asked the children for prayers of reparation for sin and intercession for sinners so that all would be saved and none would be lost. The three visionaries responded so generously to Our Lady's call. Going all the way back to the first apparition of the Angel of Peace to the children in the spring of 1916, the children had been accustomed to praying the Rosary after lunch while watching the sheep. But they generally rushed through the Rosary so they could get to their games more quickly. But after the angel's second apparition, which stressed their need for prayer and sacrifice, and then his third apparition which focused the children on Eucharistic Adoration and reparation, the children made great strides in prayer. They were assured that God and Our Lady loved them and their prayers reflected that confidence. This is an important lesson for all of us! How do we pray? With confidence? Or perhaps with distraction and indifference? Do we really believe God is listening to our prayer, or do we simply say maybe God will do something to help me. St. Thérèse, who was known for her great childlike confidence in God, once said: "You will receive from God what you expect to receive."

The Power of the Rosary

In her appeal for prayer Our Lady stressed above all the daily recitation of the Rosary. This request was the only one she made at all six of her apparitions to the visionaries at the Cova da Iria. She stressed to the children how necessary this prayer was. (The Rosary is powerful enough to stop wars, bring world peace and convert sinners!) Have we taken Our Lady's request for the daily Rosary seriously in our own lives? Or do we simply relegate it to the category of "if I have time I'll pray it?" If we really trusted in the words of Our Lady that the Rosary is so powerful, then wouldn't we make the time to pray it devoutly and daily? Don't be deterred by distractions; even the saints got distractions during the Rosary! Remember, as long as your distractions are not voluntary and your mind and imagination are simply roaming on their own, that does not break the union of your heart with God. Your heart is still praying even though your imagination is focusing elsewhere. But we should always pray with confidence because Our Lady is reassuring us of the power of her special prayer. Pray daily, making the best effort you can to say it devoutly, and it will change your life forever. It will actually be the intercession of Our Lady with her Divine Son that will bring about this change. After all, who would not have confidence in such a loving and compassionate Mother as Our Lady is?

Trust In Our Lady's Promises

Another area where trust is so important is to have confidence that the promises that Our Lady made to us at Fatima will be fulfilled. Many people have lost trust in Our Lady's message with its great promises saying that if the consecration of Russia to the Immaculate Heart of Mary was made, why is there not an era of peace in the world? Remember Saint John Paul II did his part in making the consecration of Russia with the overwhelming majority of the bishops of the Church to the Immaculate Heart of Mary as she requested. Even Sister Lucia said after the consecration, "Heaven accepted it!" … "The Holy Father did the best he could!" Could the Pope have done better than the best he could? Our Lady would not have expected that. The other part of the solution we need now is our prayers of reparation for the sins of the world and intercession for the salvation of souls. Above all we must practice the Five First Saturdays Devotion faithfully. Our Lady did say that when enough people do as she has asked at Fatima then the era of peace she promised will be given to us. We must trust Our Lady to be faithful to her promises. Ardent trust on our part will make things happen sooner on God's part. This is like Saint Peter saying in one of his letters that we should look forward to the Second Coming of Christ and try to hasten it by our longing for Him to come (cf. 2 Pt 3).

In one of her dialogues with the children, Our Lady told

them to "pray to Our Lady of the Rosary ... because she is the only one who can help you!" When Our Lady revealed her identity to the children at the last apparition in the Cova on October 13th, the time of the great Miracle of the Sun, she told the children "I am the Lady of the Rosary." If we put these two quotes together, we must conclude that Our Lady herself is the only one who can help us attain from her Divine Son the salvation of souls and the peace of the world. Always pray to Our Lady with childlike confidence. This is the confident trust we need to renew.

One of the things we must expect as we grow in our life of faith is to be tested. Testing by God is not spoken about much today but was always part of God's plan. God, for example, tested our first parents in the Garden of Eden. He tested even those who were very close to Him, like Moses and the Jewish people in the desert. Jesus tested His apostle Philip when He asked in order to feed the crowd of 5,000, "Where shall we buy bread for them to eat? (He knew well what He intended to do but He asked this to test Philip's response)" (Jn 6:5-6). But perhaps the one we think of most when it comes to a matter of testing faith is Abraham. He is even called "our father in faith." Abraham had three outstanding trials of his faith. When put to the test, and they were profound

84

trials, he remained steadfast in trusting the Lord. Our faith may someday have profound trials as well. Let us look at what Abraham endured in his testing and try to learn from his example how to remain steadfast. We shall at the same time look at the message of Our Lady of Fatima which calls us to have a faith that endures in trials similar to Abraham's.

A Trial of Facing the Unknown

The three great trials of Abraham are mentioned in Hebrews 11. The first of his trials dealt with facing the unknown. Here is what the Letter to the Hebrews says:

> "By faith Abraham obeyed when he was called, and went forth to the place he was to receive as a heritage; he went forth, moreover, not knowing where he was going" (Heb 11:8).

We find the actual call of Abraham described in chapter 12 of Genesis. We read there that the Lord said to Abraham: "Go forth from the land of your kinsfolk and from your father's house to a land that I will show you" (Gn 12:1). What seems to be such a simple directive is actually quite profound. We must stop and realize what this implied in terms of a test for Abraham. First of all, God tells him to leave his land which was called Harran. The Scriptures tell us he was 75 years old, not exactly a time when most people would begin such a new undertaking in life. To leave his land also meant to leave those things that were familiar to him. Furthermore, the Lord commanded him to leave his kinsfolk and his father's house. Not only does this mean he would leave close family and friends, but he would also leave the security that one's family and clan provided in terms of protection and support in the ancient world.

Finally, he was told to go "to a land that I will show you" (Gn 12:1). Have you ever seen "a land that I will show you" on a map? You don't know where it is, you don't know how to get there and you won't know you are there until you actually arrive. How would you like to travel like that? Yet, in a real sense all of us traveling through the journey of life do not know exactly what lies ahead of us or where we will end up. By our faith, the only thing we can hold on to is the firm conviction that God who has called us to this journey of faith will guide us. There is no doubt that Abraham left with the conviction that the God who called him would go with him, and remain with him until he got to the land that God intended to show him.

This trial of Abraham throws light especially on the aspect of the vocation or mission God calls each of us to in life. For example, someone called to the married life does not know what joys or sorrows await him or her in the future. On their wedding day they make a promise to each other before God to be faithful, and to share their lives even most intimately "until death do they part." This is a great leap of faith into the future, a journey into a land that God will show that couple in the years ahead. The traditional marriage formula used to express this idea very clearly. The priest would read to the young, starry-eyed couple in front of him these very challenging words:

> Your future life, with its joys and its sorrows, its hopes and its disappointments, its successes and its failures, is this day hidden from your eyes. But as they are

part of every human life, they are to be
expected in your own. So you are ready
to take each other for better or for worse,
for richer or for poorer, in sickness and in
health, until death do you part.

These words are certainly sobering to say the least.
Many couples might dream in terms of the many fairy-
tales they heard as children that ended with a marriage
of a handsome prince to a beautiful princess, and "they
lived happily ever after." Unfortunately, reality is not
made up of dreams. It demands the honesty to face the
commitments we make, the determination of faithfulness to abide by the promises they make, and with God's
grace to persevere to the end. Many people today reject
the notion of a lifelong commitment or of the necessity to remain with one partner. They want a "freedom"
which is simply an excuse to seek their own pleasure
on their own terms. But love demands a faithful giving.
God's love for us is faithful and so we must respond to
Him and to one another with a love that is faithful.

Even the call to the priesthood or to the religious life is
like a "going into a land I will show you." Like the command to Abraham, there is something of a mystery in the
call one hears to serve the Lord. No doubt years of preparation in the seminary or religious house of formation
help to prepare the candidates for the decision they will
make to commit their lives to God's service. But since
they do not know what those years of service will entail,
they need the faith of an Abraham to go forth, leaving
their family and familiar circumstances to embark on a
life of service to God and His people. The mystery of every Christian call implies, therefore, a readiness to meet
the tests that lie hidden in the path ahead.

Fatima and the Trial of a Call

When Our Blessed Lady made her first appearance to little Lucia, Francisco, and Jacinta in the Cova da Iria, on May 13, 1917, one of the first things she asked them was: "Will you accept suffering from God for the salvation of souls and the peace of the world?" The children had been prepared to answer this question generously by the prayers and instruction of the Angel of Peace, who had appeared to them three times in 1916. He stirred their love for God by teaching them to be faithful to their prayers and to have a generous spirit of sacrifice. This is why they so courageously responded "Yes" to Our Lady's question. They did endure many sufferings and were willing to make many sacrifices, in the land that Our Lady showed them. We too have received this call through Mary's intercession at Fatima. It is rooted in our Baptism which gave us new life in Christ. This new life must, in turn, give life to others through prayer, sacrifice, suffering, and the witness of a holy life. All of this is at the heart of Our Lady of Fatima's call to faith!

The Trial of the Test of Time

The second test of Abraham was the result of a promise God had made him. As we saw already, Abraham was 75 when he left Harran. Now he was 100 years old and Sarah is described as being 90 (cf. Gn 17:17). Yet God promised Abraham that he would have a son by his wife Sarah. Frequently God had said to Abraham that he would have descendants "as numerous as the stars in the sky and the sands of the seashore," which was the Jewish way of saying there would be so many that he could not number them. Yet he did not have even one child from his wife Sarah. It was no doubt a great test for Abraham to continue to believe that this could ever possibly happen. Here is what we read in the Letter to the Hebrews about Abraham's second test:

> "By faith Sarah received power to conceive though she was sterile and Abraham was past the age, for he thought that the One who had made the promise was worthy of trust. As a result of this faith, there came forth from one man, who was himself as good as dead, descendants as numerous as the stars in the sky and the sands of the seashore" (Heb 11:11-12).

For Abraham, this trial was the test of time, a very difficult one indeed. How often he must have wondered how and when God would fulfill His promise. But it is clear that he never doubted the promise. We, too, are often put to the test of time. Perhaps we pray for a certain blessing and it seems that it never comes. This is especially difficult when there is not even the slightest indication that our prayer and trust will be realized. For example, people pray for years for the conversion of loved ones. That conversion never seems to come. In fact, in many instances the conversion never seems any closer while in fact it may seem further away as more complications enter the situation. But still we are called to believe and not to lose hope in the promises of God. As the Angel Gabriel told Our Lady at the Annunciation: "Know that Elizabeth, your kinswoman, has conceived a son in her old age; she who was thought to be sterile is now in her sixth month, for nothing is impossible with God" (Lk 1:36-37).

We can see this test of Abraham reflected in the Fatima message as well. It has been nearly a hundred years since Our Lady came and promised in her July 1917 message to the children that, despite another world war and despite the evils that Russia would spread around the world, an era of peace would come to the world through the triumph of her Immaculate Heart. So many people today have lost confidence in the message and promise of Our Lady. So many people tell this author that they do not see peace in the world, but in fact see much more violence among nations. They ask with a certain disbelief where the promise of Our Lady is fulfilled?

I think to deal with this trial we must follow the example of Abraham. Faith is believing even when we do not see. It is a confident trust in the promises of God even though they are not yet fulfilled. Many people assume that Saint John Paul II did not consecrate Russia properly and so that is why there is no peace. This is not true. The Pope did consecrate Russia correctly or else the Soviet Union would never have fallen nor would the right to practice religion in Russia and the former Soviet Republics have been restored. What is holding up the triumph of the peace of the world is that there are not enough of us who are living holy lives, offering prayers of intercession, reparation, and sacrifices for the conversion of sinners. Above all, we must carry out faithfully the request of Jesus and His Holy Mother made at Pontevedra, Spain in 1925 to practice the Five First Saturdays Devotion. (Sister Lucia often said that the request for the Five First Saturdays Devotion is the most neglected part of the Fatima Message.) This is why Our Lady stated that when enough people have done what she asked, then the triumph of her Immaculate Heart would come and an era of peace would be given to the world. This is our test of time: to continue to believe and to be faithful in carrying out what Our Lady wants. Let us remember a wise reminder: "God may not come when we expect Him, but He is never late!"

The Trial of Sacrifice

The third and final trial for Abraham was the greatest of all. God tested him to put his whole existence on the line by offering up his only true son Isaac. Remember that at the time of Abraham there was no clear idea that a person lived after death. They believed that you lived on through your descendants who kept your memory alive. So with the command of God to sacrifice his only son Isaac, Abraham faced the prospect of his name being obliterated from the earthly book of life forever. Every hope he had was in that little son and now God was asking him to sacrifice that son. This is how the Letter to the Hebrews describes this final heartrending trial:

> "By faith, Abraham, when put to the test, offered up Isaac; he who had received the promises was ready to sacrifice his only son, of whom it was said, 'through Isaac shall your descendants be called.' He reasoned that God was able to raise from the dead, and so he received Isaac back as a symbol" (Heb 11:17-19).

Not all of us will be faced with this trial of sacrifice. Certainly, accepting the death of a loved one involves something of this trial, especially when it may be sudden and unexpected. But it is quite a different thing to actually offer up that beloved person. Didn't Our Lady herself endure this trial at the foot of the cross? After all, Jesus had said that no one could take His life from Him but that He was freely laying it down for our salvation.

> "For this reason the Father loves me, because I lay down my life, that I may take it up again. No one takes it from me, but I lay it down of my own accord. I have power to lay it down, and I have power to take it up again; this charge I have received from my Father" (Jn 10: 17-18).

Venerable Archbishop Fulton J. Sheen used to say that on the cross Jesus was offering the sacrifice of Himself for the world's salvation. On Calvary He was the Victim as the Lamb of God being offered as a sacrifice for the atonement of our sins. He was also the Priest who offered Himself in accordance with the Father's will. Standing at the foot of the cross Our Lady had to join in the sacrifice of her Son, offering Him in His sacrificial death to the Father. St. Paul reminds us that God spared Abraham's son, but not his own Son.

We must live our lives joined to the dying and the rising of Jesus. St. Paul reminds us that in our Baptism we die to our old life of sin, both Original Sin and where present personal sins as well. At Fatima Our Lady reminded us of this sacrificial aspect of our Christian call. She said we had to die to sins when she told the children at her apparition of October 13th, looking very sad, Our Lady said: "Do not offend the Lord our God anymore, because He is already so much offended." She also said we must endure our sufferings and offer our personal sacrifices and prayers, especially the Rosary, for the conversion of sinners, as when she said in her August apparition: "Pray, pray very much, and make sacrifices for sinners; for many souls go to hell, because there are none to sacrifice themselves and to pray for them."

Abraham's test was to sacrifice his only son through whom every promise made by God to have numerous descendants and to have his name remain forever had to be carried out. He was willing to offer this supreme sacrifice and God blessed him, making him father of all believers. Our Lady has warned us at Fatima that we have a choice to make and it involves a great sacrifice. If we live lives of sin and disregard her message, the spread of the evil of Communism that she warned about in her July apparition will continue to inflict great harm and suffering on the world. On the other hand, if we are willing to take the challenge of this sacrifice, we must spend our lives honoring God, doing good, offering intercession for the conversion of sinners and reparation for the offenses against Almighty God. If we are generous and faithful, the Lord will bless us. Remember Our Lady has promised that if enough people do as she has said, "in the end my Immaculate Heart will triumph." She also told the children: "I am the only one who can help you."

Chapter Four

The Mysteries of the Rosary
The Joyful Mysteries

The mysteries of the Rosary, especially with the recent addition of the Luminous Mysteries (or the Mysteries of Light), offer us a wonderful overview of the lives of Jesus and Mary. Saint John Paul II, in his beautiful letter on the Holy Rosary, stated that the Rosary is not solely a Marian prayer, but also a Christocentric prayer. He called it a "compendium of the Gospel." Every time we meditate on the mysteries of the Rosary, the lives of Jesus and Mary with their virtues and perfect fulfillment of the will of God the Father, guide us along the road to holiness. At the same time, the Holy Spirit is forming Christ in us so that He can live His mysteries once again through each one of us.

The Joyful Mysteries

Family life with marriage, birth of children, years of infancy and childhood serve as the foundation for the rest of our lives. In this sense the Joyful Mysteries serve as the "take-off" for our own family lives because they focus us on the virtues and trials of Jesus, Mary and Joseph, the holiest of all families. The memories of family, childhood experiences and the wonder of children looking at the world are often treasured. At the same time, they can set the course for the rest of one's life. As we reflect on the Joyful Mysteries, we will find in the events surrounding the birth of Jesus and His early life, great insights into Christian family life and the importance of childhood formation in the faith.

The Annunciation

In this mystery we reflect on the greatest event in human history: the Son of God became Man. God the Father so loved the world He gave His only Son to be our Redeemer and source of new life. Corresponding to this infinite act of love by God the Father giving us His own Divine Son, there had to be a fitting response on the part of mankind. Our Blessed Lady offered this response to God's invitation. When the archangel Gabriel announced to Mary that she was to conceive a Son who would be the Savior of the world, she responded with loving trust and total abandonment: "Behold, I am the handmaid of the Lord. May it be done to me according to your word" (Lk 1:38). At that moment the Word became Flesh and the world would no longer ever be the same. In this mystery let us ask Our Blessed Lady to obtain for us the grace to be always ready to do God's will in our daily lives.

The Visitation

After Our Blessed Mother learned from the archangel that her aged cousin Elizabeth was with child, she went in haste to be of assistance. As soon as Our Lady spoke to her aged cousin, the child in the womb of Elizabeth, St. John the Baptist, leapt for joy. Mary had brought the presence of Christ her Son to both mother and child. Whenever Our Lady comes, she always brings the presence of Christ, her Son, into the lives of those she encounters. Let us ask Our Blessed Lady in this mystery to obtain for us also the grace that we may bring the love of Christ her Son to all those we meet in daily life.

The Birth of Jesus

In this mystery we meditate on the awesome event of the birth of Jesus. From all eternity Jesus is the Son of God by His Divinity; now, in time, He also became the Son of Mary by His humanity. In becoming man Jesus emptied Himself of His divine glory and hid it behind the humble form of a child. It is Christ, born for us as Savior, who gives us every treasure of heaven and earth. Relying only on ourselves, we would have nothing but our sins. In this mystery let us ask Our Blessed Lady and Saint Joseph to obtain for us a child-like spirit so that we may come to know Jesus born in poverty and humility for our sake, in order that He might enrich our lives with His grace and love.

The Presentation of the Child Jesus in the Temple

Two people met the child Jesus when He was presented in the temple by Mary and Joseph, forty days after His birth. One was an aged man named Simeon who had been awaiting the coming of the Messiah. Inspired by the Holy Spirit that he would live to see the promised Child, he was moved by the same Spirit to come to the temple precisely at the moment Jesus was presented. Taking the Child Jesus into his arms, Simeon prayed with profound gratitude: "Now, Master, You may let Your servant go in peace... for my eyes have seen Your salvation" (Lk 2:29-30). He proclaimed Jesus as the Light of the Nations and the Glory of Israel. He then turned to Our Lady and said: "This child is destined for the fall and rise of many in Israel.... And you yourself a sword will pierce" (Lk 2:34-35).

The second person to encounter the Child Jesus was an aged woman named Anna, who had spent her many years of widowhood praying and fasting in the temple. "She gave thanks to God and spoke about the Child to all who were awaiting the redemption of Jerusalem" (Lk 2:38).

Let us ask Our Lady and Saint Joseph in this mystery to help us encounter Christ both in moments when we are consciously awaiting Him and even in moments when He comes unexpectedly. At the same time, let us ask in this mystery to be ready to share the joys and sorrows of Jesus, in order to grow in understanding, more and more, of who He is and that we might feel the effects of His redemption in our daily lives.

The Finding of Jesus in the Temple

In this mystery we contemplate how Jesus at the age of twelve became separated from Mary and Joseph as they were returning to Nazareth after visiting the temple in Jerusalem. Mary and Joseph seek the child Jesus in great sorrow and rejoice to find Him on the third day. Our Lady asks her Son: "Why have you done this to us? Your father [Saint Joseph] and I have been looking for You with great anxiety." Jesus answers His mother: "Why were you looking for Me? Did you not know that I must be in my Father's house?" [His Heavenly Father] (Lk 2:48-49). Mary does not immediately understand the mystery that Jesus is presenting to her – the demands of His love for the Father come even above family ties.

Many times we, too, experience a sense of separation when we do not feel the presence of God, as we go through trials and darkness in our lives. In this mystery let us ask Our Lady and Saint Joseph to make us strong and courageous as we experience life's trials. They will remind us that the Lord is always with us even at times when He may seem far away. Let us also ask that we may always continue to seek Jesus until we find Him and never give up.

The Mysteries of the Rosary
The Luminous Mysteries

The Luminous Mysteries, also known as the Mysteries of Light, were a special blessing given to the Church by Saint John Paul II. As the Holy Father was beginning the 25th anniversary of his Pontificate on October 16, 2002, he published an Apostolic Letter *"Rosarium Virginis Mariae"* (RVM). In his letter he proclaimed the "Year of the Rosary" to last from October 2002 to October, 2003. He also introduced five new mysteries which refer to the public life of Our Lord. They actually filled in an apparent "gap" in the mysteries of the Rosary because previously we went from Jesus' childhood and hidden life in the Joyful Mysteries immediately to His passion and death in the Sorrowful Mysteries. The Luminous Mysteries have, therefore, made our reflections on the life of Jesus and His Holy Mother complete.

When writing of these mysteries in his Apostolic Letter, Saint John Paul II calls them "Mysteries of Light" because "each of these mysteries is a revelation of the Kingdom now present in the very person of Jesus" (par #21). The whole mystery of Christ, the Pope said, is a mystery of light because Christ is the Light of the world.

The Baptism of the Lord

The baptism of Jesus is the first Mystery of Light. It marks the beginning of His public life and mission. Jesus was about to leave the anonymity of His hidden family life in Nazareth. He would be revealed at His baptism in the Jordan both in His relationship to the Father and the Holy Spirit, as well as, in regard to His mission as the Savior of the world. Until now, Jesus had been known as "the son of Mary" and "the carpenter's son" from Nazareth. At His baptism He would be acknowledged before all by His Heavenly Father: "This is my Beloved Son, with Whom I am well pleased" (Mt 3:17). He would also be revealed as the Christ, the Anointed One, when the Spirit of God descended like a dove and rested upon Him (cf. Jn 1:32). The Holy Spirit, often referred to by the scriptural title "the Oil of Gladness" (cf. Heb 1:9), anoints Jesus for His mission as the Messiah. As the prophet Isaiah had foretold: "The Spirit of the Lord is upon me because the Lord has anointed me" (Is 61-1).

The fact that Jesus was baptized at all reveals something of His role as our Savior.

John's baptism was a ritual for sinners to repent of their sins and prepare to receive the Messiah. Jesus had no sins! He was holiness itself! Even St. John tried to dissuade Jesus: "I need to be baptized by you, and yet you are coming to me?" (Mt 3:14). The waters did not cleanse Jesus; Jesus cleansed the waters. He would later give to the waters the power to take away sins in the name of the Trinity in His sacrament of Baptism.

Jesus' Self-Manifestation by His Miracle at Cana

The second Mystery of Light occurs in the setting of a wedding feast. There was a true wedding celebration at Cana, but there is hardly any reference to who the bride and groom were. What actually takes place is that Jesus works His first "sign" or miracle by changing about 150 gallons of water into "choice wine." The miracle was worked through the intercession of Our Blessed Lady: "They have no wine" (Jn 2:3). By His first miracle, Jesus reveals His glory and His disciples believe in Him. In a spiritual sense, the wedding feast of Cana can be seen as a "mystical marriage" between Christ, the Divine Bridegroom, and the Church, His Bride, represented by Our Lady and the first disciples. We also see Mary's powerful intercession as Mother of the Church, always attentive to our needs. Through her intercession, God's blessings are always abundant; there was a lot of wine! But she is still reminding us: "Do whatever my Son tells you" (Jn 2:5).

Proclamation of the Gospel and Call to Conversion

After Jesus reveals His glory and the first disciples believe in Him, Jesus began to publicly proclaim His basic message of salvation: "The Kingdom of God is at hand! Repent, and believe in the Gospel!" (cf. Mk 1:15). Jesus here reveals Himself in terms of the servant of the Lord whom the prophet Isaiah had foretold would go about bringing abundant blessings to God's people (cf. Is 61:1-2). In the synagogue at Nazareth Jesus actually revealed Himself in terms of that prophecy: "The Spirit of the Lord is upon me, because He has anointed me to bring glad tidings to the poor. He has sent me to proclaim liberty to captives and recovery of sight to the blind, to let the oppressed go free, and to proclaim a year acceptable to the Lord" (Lk 4:18-19). By word and deed Jesus was revealing the Kingdom. He would be the New Lawgiver. As we pray this Luminous Mystery let us remember that we are called to be witnesses for Jesus today. This is the mission of the New Evangelization. Essential to that mission is the call to repentance, acknowledging our sins and seeking God's mercy in the Sacrament of Reconciliation.

The Transfiguration of Jesus

Saint John Paul II said that the Transfiguration is the Mystery of Light par excellence. He wrote in his Apostolic Letter: "The glory of the Godhead shines forth from the face of Christ as the Father commands the astonished apostles to 'listen to Him'" (Lk 9:35). St. Paul had said: "He emptied Himself taking the form of a slave, coming in human likeness; and found in human appearance, He humbled Himself…." (Phil 2:7-8). For one moment Jesus allowed His hidden glory to be manifested. So overwhelming was this moment of joy and ecstasy that St. Peter remarks: "Lord, it is good that we are here. If you wish, I will make three tents here, one for you, one for Moses, and one for Elijah" (Mt 17:4). He did not want this moment to end! But in life our ecstasies are only temporary. They prepare us to spiritually share in the agony of Jesus' passion as Peter, James and John later did. Ultimately, however, they give us the courage and hope to look forward to the unending joy of the Resurrection and a life transfigured by the Holy Spirit.

The Institution of the Eucharist

The final Mystery of Light occurs at the Last Supper. Jesus changes bread and wine into His very Body and Blood. He had foretold the gift of the Eucharist during

His discourse on the Bread of Life (cf. Jn 6). He had proclaimed Himself "the Living Bread that came down from Heaven" (Jn 6:51) and promised to feed us with His flesh and blood. He told His disciples that He eagerly desired to eat this Passover meal with them so that He might become their very food and drink (cf. Lk 22:15). Through this gift Jesus reveals Himself as the One who sustains us. Through receiving Him in the Eucharist, He continues to live His earthly life and mission in each one of us again. As our Eucharistic love grows, we come to know Jesus. In this life we shall never be able to totally comprehend the love that He shows us in His beautiful gift of Himself in the Eucharist. As Ven. Archbishop Fulton J. Sheen once expressed it: "The greatest love story of all time is contained in a tiny white Host!"

St. Alphonsus Mary Liguori says that the person who wants to grow in loving God can find no better topic to meditate on than the sufferings that Jesus endured for us on the cross. When we think that He was God who became Man, and was willing to undergo sufferings that we deserved because of our sins, we cannot help but be deeply moved with sentiments of gratitude, love and the desire to give our all in return. No wonder St. Francis de Sales called Mount Calvary "the hill of lovers." Meditation on Jesus' sorrows and sufferings moves us to experience with St. Paul, "The love of Christ impels us …" (2 Cor 5:14) to give our love completely in return.

Three Graces

St. Alphonsus tells us that Jesus gives three graces to souls. Meditating on the Sorrowful Mysteries can help us respond to them very effectively. The first grace is to stop sinning. Our Lady told the children at Fatima, tell the people to "not offend the Lord our God any more, because He is already so much offended." Many people stop sinning because they fear God's punishment. Meditating on Jesus' sufferings moves us even more to reform our lives for love of God. The second grace is to do good things. These include growing in prayer (e.g. daily Rosary, frequent Mass, regular Confession) and increasing our practice of the corporal and spiritual works of mercy (e.g. feeding the hungry, visiting the sick, instructing the ignorant). The third grace is to endure trials and sufferings patiently. This is the hardest thing for us because suffering of any kind – physical, emotional, spiritual – is repugnant to our frail human nature. As Jesus said: "The spirit is willing but the flesh is weak" (Mk 14:38). One of the secrets of the saints is that they found the strength and even the willingness to endure their sufferings patiently by reflecting on the sufferings Jesus endured so lovingly for us.

The Agony in the Garden

Jesus had often gathered in the Garden of Gethsemane with His disciples. Now it would be different. Three of them – Peter, James and John – had been with Him on another mountain, Tabor. They had seen Jesus transformed in glory and they did not want the ecstasy to end. "Lord it is good that we are here! Let us make three tents" (Mk 9:5). Little did they know it would prepare them for the agony Jesus was now enduring in the Garden. God also strengthens us in moments of our trials by consolations in prayer or through others. Often anguish in one's soul can be more painful than bodily sufferings. Undoubtedly, Jesus' anguish was unfathomable. "When He arrived at the place He said to (His disciples), 'Pray that you may not undergo the test.' After withdrawing about a stone's throw from them, and kneeling, He prayed, saying, 'Father, if You are willing, take this cup away from Me; still, not My will but Yours be done.' And to strengthen Him, an angel from heaven appeared to Him. He was in such agony and He prayed so fervently that His sweat became like drops of blood falling on the ground" (Lk 22:40-44). We can assume that the Lord foresaw the sufferings He would undergo. His very body seemed to recoil from what awaited Him, but He remained faithful to the Father's Will. We, too, recoil from the sufferings we foresee in life. We can take courage from Our Lord's own example and ask Him, through the merits of His sufferings, for the grace to be faithful, despite our weakness, and accept the Father's Will as best we can. God will often send us an "angel," to console and encourage us in the midst of our trials.

The Scourging At the Pillar

Pilate, bowing to the pressure of the crowd which demanded Jesus' death, had Our Lord scourged. What a terrible suffering! Undoubtedly, the innocent body of Christ was far more sensitive to pain than our own. Yet the cruel executioners literally covered Our Lord's body with scourges which can still be seen on the Shroud of Turin.

Why did Jesus undergo such excruciating suffering? Probably to atone for our sins of the flesh, Jesus allowed

His body to suffer. The sins of impurity which dishonor the body as a temple of the Holy Spirit could only be atoned for by the sufferings of the body of Christ. Our Lady of Fatima told little Jacinta, "More souls are lost from God by sins of impurity than by any other sins." We must implore the merits of Jesus from His scourging to practice chastity according to our state in life. We must also pray that through these same merits those who are prisoners of lust will be set free.

Jesus Is Crowned with Thorns

Jesus had claimed before Pilate to be a King, but not of this world. As a result, the Roman soldiers treated Jesus as a mock King. "Weaving a crown out of thorns, they placed it on His head, and a reed in His right hand. And kneeling before Him, they mocked Him, saying, 'Hail, King of the Jews!' They spat upon Him and took the reed and kept striking Him on the head" (Mt 27:29-30). It seems incredible that the God-man, Jesus Christ, would allow Himself to be mocked by His own creatures, especially when we realize that with one thought, He could have wiped the entire Roman army off the face of the earth! What humility the God-man teaches us. "Come to me, all you who labor and are burdened, and I will give you rest. Take my yoke upon you and learn from Me, for I am meek and humble of heart; and you will find rest for yourselves. For my yoke is easy, and my burden light" (Mt 11:28-30).

Jesus Carries the Cross

Roman practice required that those condemned to die by crucifixion had to carry their own cross to the place of execution. Jesus carried His up to Mount Calvary.

As we meditate on Jesus making His way, we are encouraged to bear our share of the cross. This was a requirement to be Jesus' disciple. "Whoever wishes to come after me must deny himself, take up his cross and follow me" (Mk 8:34). Ven. Archbishop Sheen used to say that the two beams of our cross are made up of our responsibilities toward God and our neighbor. The vertical beam consists of our struggles to be faithful in loving and serving the Lord. The horizontal beam is comprised of our efforts to love our neighbor as Jesus loved us. These are the trials of patience, kindness, sharing, and especially forgiveness.

The Stations of the Cross is a very important Catholic devotion. Some of the Stations are found in Scripture while others are not. Meditating on this fourth Sorrowful Mystery, we can see ourselves like a Simon of Cyrene helping Jesus to carry His cross in the needs and sufferings of His least brothers and sisters, or like the women weeping over Jesus' sufferings by repenting of our sins which caused Jesus to suffer. Of the other traditional Stations not found in the Gospel, we can pray to meet Mary in our daily journey of following Jesus on the Via Dolorosa, or else we can be like a St. Veronica who offered her veil to Jesus to wipe the blood and sweat from His face. In gratitude, the Lord left His countenance on her veil; Jesus will leave His spiritual image on our hearts.

The Crucifixion and Death of the Lord

Without doubt, the greatest act of love the world has ever seen was the death of Jesus on Good Friday. As St. Peter expressed it, "The Author of life you put to death…" (Acts 3:15). Ven. Archbishop Sheen used to say that Jesus was the only one ever born into this world in order to die. His death was the price of our redemption. Jesus' enemies mocked Him saying, "Let Him come down from the cross now and we will believe in Him" (Mt 27:42). If Jesus had come down and not died, we would not have been saved. "Dying, You destroyed our death; rising, You restored our life; Lord Jesus, come in glory."

The cross was to be Jesus' last and greatest pulpit. His "seven last words" are among the most profound He ever uttered. He prayed for forgiveness, placed us in the care of His mother, endured a feeling of abandonment by His Heavenly Father, and thirsted for our love and salvation. In all these sufferings Jesus gained eternal life for us. The cross which the Romans created to be the instrument of torture and degradation has become, through the suffering of Christ upon it, the instrument of our salvation. The cross is the "new tree of life!"

Every earthly journey must have an ending. How much time, money and effort is spent planning our journeys well, so that we end up in the right place with the best possible accommodations. What applies to our earthly journeys applies even more so to our heavenly journey. Our whole life on earth should be lived with the heavenly ending of our journey in view. As one person put it years ago, "We are all on a collision course with God and we need to get ready for the impact!"

Our earthly journeys can end up anywhere in this world. We sometimes see airline ads that say, for example: "We have 525 destinations in 125 countries." That can be very impressive! The spiritual journey, on the other hand, doesn't have quite so many possible destinations. In fact, in the final analysis there are only two: heaven or hell!

110

Like a "pass" or "fail" grade, we will end up in one of these two eternal destinations. Leading up to these are two other experiences we must all pass through, namely, death and judgment. If you put all four of these experiences together, you get what are called the "Four Last Things," namely, death, judgment, heaven and hell.

Saint John Paul II used to stress the need for Catholics to reflect on the four last things so that they will always keep in mind where they are headed. It is like the story of a famous absent-minded professor who was about to board a train. He was searching his suit and pants pockets in vain for his ticket. When the conductor realized the man's dilemma and that a crowd was forming behind him, he told the professor: "It's obvious you cannot find your ticket, I'm sure you're an honest man. So why don't you just get on the train and when you find your ticket, show it to me later." But the professor said: "I can't do that! I can't get on the train until I find my ticket! I have to remember where I'm going!" On our spiritual journey, we all need to remember where we're going! The glorious mysteries help us to do this, because they shed light on what lies beyond the veil of death. When we meditate on them as we pray the Rosary, they can become a great support to our hope to share eternal life with our Lord and Savior, Jesus Christ, and His Blessed Mother!

The Resurrection: Jesus' Victory over Sin and Death

The death of Jesus Christ was a saving death. He did not die helpless before the power of the Jewish Sanhedrin or of the Roman procurator, Pontius Pilate. With one thought of His mind, He could have wiped the entire Roman army off the face of the earth! But rather, He meekly submitted to great suffering and an ignominious death on the cross because it was His Heavenly Father's will for our salvation. He became the Lamb of God whose sacrificial death would take away the sins of the world. But His victory would not have been complete if He remained in death, because death was the punishment for sin. So Jesus in a sense submitted to the power and chains of death by dying, but then destroyed that power and broke those chains both for Himself and for us by rising again on Easter Sunday!

In Chapter 15 of his First Letter to the Corinthians, St. Paul speaks about the importance of the resurrection of Jesus. He said the risen Lord was seen by many witnesses who testified to the reality of the resurrection! He also emphasized that if Christ was not raised from the dead, then neither will we be raised from the dead! (After all, who would raise us up if Christ was still dead?) It would mean that our faith would be worthless because we would still be in our sins! But St. Paul emphasizes that just as in Adam all died, so in Christ all will come to life again! By His resurrection Jesus has triumphed over death; at His final coming Jesus will raise us up to share His victory of eternal life! This made the Apostle exclaim: "Death is swallowed up in victory! O death, where is your victory? O death, where is your sting?" (1 Cor 15: 54-55). Fittingly, then, did St. Augustine describe Christians as "Easter people."

When we pray this first Glorious Mystery, let us ask the Lord that we may come to know the power of His resurrection (cf. Phil 3:10). This includes our hope to share in Jesus' bodily resurrection by our own on the last day, as well as a confident trust that if Jesus could conquer sin and death for us, then He can help us to overcome any trial or difficulty we may meet with along the journey to eternal life.

The Ascension: Jesus Enters His Heavenly Glory

For a period of 40 days after Easter, the risen Lord Jesus appeared to many of His disciples to confirm in them the belief in His bodily resurrection. On the 40th day He ascended into heaven to take His place of glory at His Heavenly Father's right hand! On earth Jesus had perfectly fulfilled the Will of His Heavenly Father, which included humiliation, suffering and death on a cross. Now in heaven, Jesus was glorified by His Heavenly Father. This formed part of Jesus' Paschal Mystery, which consisted of His death, resurrection and glorification. He was first glorified in heaven by His ascension; He would later be glorified on earth by sending the Holy Spirit upon His Church on Pentecost.

When we meditate on this second Glorious Mystery, we can reflect on many other reasons besides His glorification for which Jesus ascended into heaven. He said He was going away to prepare a place for us in His Heavenly Father's house for there were many mansions there (cf. Jn 14:2). Likewise, He was going to intercede for us before His Heavenly Father's throne, offering Him the Precious Blood He shed as the price of our salvation (cf. Rom 8:34). He had to go to the Father so that He could send the Holy Spirit to His disciples (cf. Jn 15:26; 16:7). Finally, Jesus' ascending into Heaven would make us long to be with Him, much as separation makes the heart grow fonder, and thus to seek the things of heaven and not of earth (cf. Col 3:1-2).

The Descent of the Holy Spirit on Pentecost

Pentecost is truly "the birthday of the Church." On Pentecost the Holy Spirit descended upon our Blessed Mother, the twelve apostles and Jesus' first disciples who had gathered in the upper room for nine days of prayer to receive the Gift of God (Acts 2:1-4). Jesus had promised to send the Holy Spirit to His apostles so that He could help them grasp what He [Jesus] had taught them, and to give them courage to endure the many persecutions and sufferings that would come as they proclaimed Christ to the very ends of the earth. This is why we see the apostles, who had been so fearful on Holy Thursday night, publicly proclaiming Christ with courage and conviction after Pentecost and even rejoicing to suffer for Him when they were scourged (cf. Acts 5:40-42).

As we pray this third Glorious Mystery, we should pray for the Holy Spirit to come to us personally to help us understand all that Jesus has taught us, as well as how to accomplish our Heavenly Father's Will with great love and faithfulness. We should pray for courage to live our faith without fear or shame, and to defend it appropriately when it may be questioned or attacked. Finally, we should ask our Heavenly Father and Jesus to send the Holy Spirit once again upon the whole Church to renew it in faith and fervor in these challenging times we live in. It is through the work of the Holy Spirit and the witness we give by leading good Christian lives that Jesus is glorified on earth as He is already glorified in heaven.

The Assumption of Mary, Body and Soul into Heaven

When Our Lady's earthly life was ended, she was assumed body and soul into heaven. No sin, whether original or personal, had ever touched her soul. She always did all that God asked of her, this faithful "handmaid of the Lord," even when it meant that swords of sorrow would pierce her Immaculate Heart! After all, it was from her that Jesus took His very humanity, His flesh and blood, by which He lived among us and carried out the work of our redemption. He later gave them to us as our Eucharistic food and drink. In the profound mystery of the Incarnation, we come to realize that Mary was the only creature whoever gave God something He did not have! It is not surprising, then, that in His great love for His Blessed Mother, Jesus took her body and soul into heaven so that no corruption would ever touch her body.

As we meditate on this fourth Glorious Mystery, we realize that in Mary, Jesus has given us a marvelous example of His saving power. By her privilege of the Immaculate Conception, Jesus shows us His power to redeem us from sin for Mary had no sin at all! By her privilege of the Assumption, Jesus shows His power to free us from bodily death! We can see in Our Lady, then, what the whole Church will someday be: the sinless and immortal bride of Christ! As we pray this mystery, let us ask Our Lady to obtain for us the grace of final perseverance in the love and service of her divine Son. Let us ask her to keep us from committing any mortal sin which is the only thing that could ever separate us from Jesus! It will then be our joy to share in the glorious victory of Jesus and Mary forever!

The Crowning of Mary as Queen of Heaven and Earth

In biblical times it was generally the mother of the king who was given the title of "queen." This was because many kings at the time had more than one wife; but they each had only one mother! So Mary, as the Mother of Jesus our King, is honored as the Queen! Since Jesus is King of heaven and earth, so Mary is Queen of heaven and earth! Because of her central role in the mystery of the Incarnation and the work of the Redemption of the world, we offer Mary a unique praise called "hyper-dulia." We do not adore Our Lady, because adoration can be given to God alone. But we do have special honor and love for her. We are grateful for all she did and suffered in the work of redemption! At the same time we are fulfilling her divine Son's words on the cross: "Woman, behold your son!... Behold your mother!"

This fifth Glorious Mystery reminds us that devout Catholics are instinctively moved to go to Mary with filial love and confidence, as little children would go to their earthly mothers! They know from experience that just like the queen-mother in the ancient world was the power behind the throne, so Mary exercises a tremendous intercessory role for her children in all their needs, both physical and spiritual. That is why many theologians see Our Lady's queenship in heaven as not only a symbol of the honor we owe her, but also of the role she plays as a mediatrix of all graces won by her Son in the redemption of the world. As the beautiful prayer, the Memorare, reminds us: "Remember, O most gracious Virgin Mary, that never was it known that anyone who fled to your protection, implored your help or sought your intercession, was left unaided..."

CHAPTER FIVE

THE CHRISTIAN MEANING OF SUFFERING IN THE LIGHT OF THE MESSAGE OF FATIMA THE MEANING OF SUFFERING IN TODAY'S WORLD

The Problem of Suffering

Years ago I came across a book entitled "The Problem of God." I remember thinking to myself: "But God does not have any problems!" The same cannot be said of "the problem of suffering." Again, God does not have a problem with it [remember, He has no problems], but we humans do! After all, suffering is something we experience and endure in one form or another every day. It can range

117

from simple annoyance at the temperature being too hot or too cold, all the way up to the tragic effects of an automobile accident or even war. Many of our sufferings are caused by other human beings, as in the case of theft or abuse. On the other hand, nature brings many sufferings such as the destruction caused by a tornado or a flood. Finally, there is the ultimate personal suffering that every human must experience, and that is bodily death.

When we try to fathom the problem of suffering, many questions immediately arise. One of the first questions deals with the very basis of the problem: "Why do we have to suffer in the first place?" Another way of stating this question is: "Did God always intend suffering to have a place in human history?" Let's reflect on this question for a few moments because it serves as a basis for the whole problem.

Suffering Is Linked to Original Sin

We need to go back to the very beginning of humanity as seen in sacred Scripture.

Our first parents were created free from all evil or suffering. They enjoyed perfect peace and harmony. According to St. Augustine's famous definition, "Peace is the tranquility of order." When everything is in order, there is peace! Before the Original Sin, everything was in order in the Garden of Eden. That is why Adam and Eve enjoyed perfect peace in every aspect of their lives. They had peace with God, seen in the fact that they conversed with him very familiarly. They had peace with one another because, despite their nakedness, they were not ashamed in each other's presence. Finally, they were at peace with all creation, since Adam would be able to work at keeping the garden and he would not experience the burden of hard labor, while Eve would be able to bear children without pain.

But when they committed the Original Sin, the impact of that sin brought great disorder into their relationships. Adam, for example, hid from God because he felt guilty. Adam and Eve hid from each other because they were now ashamed of their nakedness. And God would pass sentence on Adam such that his work in the field would now be by the sweat of his brow, while Eve would bear children in great pain. Finally, the greatest suffering of all is that God said they would have to endure bodily death as a punishment for their sin. These sufferings would now become part of human history.

Suffering Has Always Been Difficult to Endure

Human suffering, no matter what form it takes, has always been a burden for men and women to endure in their lifetime. People have dealt with the problem of suffering in many ways. When Jesus came, He willingly endured the cross of suffering. He did this primarily as a vicarious atonement for our sins. (Vicarious means that the greater part of the punishment we deserved in this world Jesus took upon Himself. He stood in our place). In other words, the sufferings of Jesus' life, especially the cross and His death upon it, were willed by His Heavenly Father as the means by which He would atone for or make up for the debt of our sins.

A second reason why Jesus suffered was to give us an example of how to endure sufferings in our own lives. His humble submission to the will of His Heavenly Father, even when this meant He would endure suffering, inspires us to accept God's will in regard to suffering in our own lives. Jesus experienced hunger and thirst, the cold and the heat. He also experienced rejection and opposition from enemies, as well as disappointment from the weaknesses and at times a lack of courage among his friends. His sufferings made us aware that our sufferings, when spiritually joined to His, become redemptive for us as well as for conversion of others.

Human Suffering Can Have Various Purposes

When God permits suffering in our life, He may allow those sufferings for various reasons. For example, many times He allows sufferings which are beneficial for our spiritual purification. Because suffering is painful to our fallen human nature, which likes pleasant things, the pain endured in suffering forces us to overcome any selfish tendency toward pleasures that are sinful. This can come in the form of resisting temptations, of breaking habits of sin or in letting go of those persons, places and things which generally lead us into wrong. We call these the "occasions of sin." G. K. Chesterton once said, "It is a good thing for a Christian to get into a lot of hot water! It keeps him clean!"

Sometimes suffering is a preventive means to keep us from greater harm in our lives. For example, how many disappointments that we endure in life cause us suffering at the moment we go through them, but later on we recognize they kept us from situations that could have been a greater evil. Such would be the case of someone who did not get a job they had their heart set on, but which God foresaw would lead them to compromise their faith or morals. But by the hand of God they found another job, later on, that allowed them to live their Christian life without compromise.

Another form of suffering would be co-redemptive suffering. This is when we endure sufferings in our own lives in union with the sufferings of Jesus for the salvation of the world. St. Paul speaks about this form of suffering in his letter to the Colossians (1:24): "Now I rejoice in my sufferings for your sake, and in my flesh I am filling up what is lacking in the afflictions of Christ on behalf of His Body, which is the Church." In other words, St. Paul saw in his sufferings an opportunity to join with Christ in making atonement for the sins of the world, thereby winning the grace of conversion for sinners. This is in the same way that St. Padre Pio would speak about his own sufferings: "Jesus wants my sufferings, Jesus needs my sufferings."

The Lord could redeem the whole world all on His own, but He chose to do it in union with each one of us. For example, Jesus could have fed the crowds without the five loaves of bread the little boy gave him. But he chose to make Himself dependent on that little boy's generous offer. So Jesus makes Himself dependent on the limited sufferings we can offer but He multiplies them by joining them to His own sufferings.

Suffering Is Important to the Fatima Message

As we shall see in the following articles, suffering plays a major part in the Fatima message. It is meant to achieve the three purposes we have just mentioned. Mary knows that our sufferings can purify us from sin and selfishness. She also knows that suffering and sacrifice will prevent many evils from coming upon the world such as war and hatred. Finally, she is requesting our sufferings and sacrifices so that many souls will be saved and there will be peace in the world.

121

The Christian Meaning of Suffering in the Light of the Message of Fatima
The World Needs the Gift of Sacrifice

Imagine living in a world where there was no love. There would be no caring, no sharing, no forgetfulness of one's self in reaching out to others. It would be a very cold and hard world. The reason is that love is the key to bringing joy and peace to other people. But love, to be true and lasting, requires an ability to forget one's self. This is why St. Thérèse, the Little Flower, in her great wisdom said, "The food of real love is sacrifice." And because the world today seems to be filling up more and more with selfishness and a narcissistic preoccupation with one's own pleasure and comfort, it seems the world needs sacrifice now more than in any other time in history.

What Is Sacrifice?

Sacrifice can take many forms, but it always has as its primary element the act of giving up or surrendering something or someone. In the New Testament, Jesus is our Eternal High Priest. St. Paul tells us that as man He is the mediator between the Trinity and the Church (1 Timothy 2: 4-5). As priest, He offered a sacrifice to take away our sins. But He was also the victim who was offered as the price of our redemption. This is why we call Jesus' saving death the sacrifice of the cross. This is why we also refer to its sacramental renewal in the Mass as the Holy Sacrifice of the Mass.

Jesus gave Himself for our sake. In our vocation as Christians we are called to give ourselves in sacrifice as well. We first give ourselves to the Lord by spending our lives, not on selfish pursuits, but to honor Him by doing His will in all things. We also then are called to sacrifice ourselves on behalf of our neighbor. At times it may cost us a great deal, but it is a sign of the greatest love. "No greater love can one have than to lay down his life for his friends" (Jn 15:13).

Share with Others

Sacrifice may sometimes be in terms of material things we give for the sake of others as when we give alms for the poor. We have to surrender something that we ourselves may have wanted, but we do it out of love. At other times we must give ourselves in service, assisting those who are in need. Jesus pointed out the needs of our brothers and sisters when He shared with us His teaching on the works of mercy. But in order to make these sacrifices we must be willing to let go of our own wants so
124

as to share with others. "Anyone who wishes to save his life will lose it" (Lk 9:24). The selfish person who never gives anything away will end up in the end spiritually bankrupt. He or she will have nothing to present to Jesus when they meet Him at the end of their earthly journey. "But the one who loses his life for My sake, will find it" (Ibid). What we have sacrificed in love and service to others the Lord will give back to us a hundredfold at the moment we encounter Him at our judgment.

Sacrifice Is a Key to the Fatima Message

The importance of sacrifice was brought home to the three little visionaries at Fatima, Lucia dos Santos, Francisco and Jacinta Marto by an angel who called himself the Angel of Portugal, the Angel of Peace. He made three appearances to the children. During the first appearance he had taught the children to pray the Pardon Prayer for the conversion of sinners:

"My God, I believe, I adore, I hope and I love You! I beg pardon for those who do not believe, do not adore, do not hope and do not love You."

He asked the children to pray this prayer very often. But when he made his second appearance around the height of summer, 1916, the children were relaxing in the shade of the trees during the siesta hours. Suddenly they saw the angel right beside them. He said to them: "What are you doing? Pray! Pray very much! The Hearts of Jesus and Mary have designs of mercy on you. Offer prayers and sacrifices constantly to the Most High."

Little Lucia responded to the angel by asking him how they were to make sacrifices. The angel explained to them:

"Make of everything you can a sacrifice, and offer it to God as an act of reparation for the sins by which He is offended, and in supplication for the conversion of sinners. You will thus draw down peace upon your country."

Along with the sufferings that God would send them, the sacrifices that they would voluntarily and generously offer would be absolutely necessary for the salvation of souls.

Offering Sacrifice

We might apply this understanding of sacrifice in two ways. First it would apply to all our thoughts, words, and actions that we do throughout the day. This is what we do when we make our morning offering.

The second form of sacrifice is even more powerful. This is to give up something that costs us by way of surrendering our convenience or attachments. These were the sacrifices Our Lady asked for during her July 13th apparition. She taught the children a prayer to say whenever they had some sacrifice to offer to God. It is called the "Sacrifice Prayer":

"Oh Jesus, it is for love of You, for the conversion of sinners, and in reparation for the sins committed against the Immaculate Heart of Mary."

The little shepherd children learned to be very generous in making their sacrifices. Sometimes they deprived themselves of tasty food and shared it with others who were poor. They learned to make a sacrifice of so many things. At the end of her life little Jacinta made a great sacrifice. After seeing Our Lady at Fatima, she so longed to go to Heaven. But Our Lady appeared to her and made her an offer, telling Jacinta she could come to Heaven immediately or remain on earth for the sake of saving souls. In her generosity little Jacinta chose to deprive herself of the joy of Heaven for the salvation of others. After six months Our Lady appeared to her and soon after took her to Heaven. Our Lady told her that many souls were saved because of her sacrifice.

Love Makes Sacrifice Easy

We know from our human experience that it is not easy to make sacrifices. We often may intend to make a sacrifice of something, and offer it to God for the salvation of souls and in reparation for sin. But sometimes we easily find reasons to excuse ourselves from making that sacrifice. That is why the spirit of sacrifice requires a great love. The children of Fatima grew to a great love. They had generous hearts.

Perhaps we can end this reflection on sacrifice with words taken from the traditional "Exhortation Before Marriage" which the priest used to read to every couple on their wedding day, before the changes in the marriage ritual after Vatican II. The priest reminded the young couple that their marriage would bind them together for life and influence their whole future. He told them that their future "with its hopes and its disappointments, its successes and its failures, its pleasures and its pains, its joys and its sorrows," were that day hidden from their eyes. But since they were part of every human life the young couple should expect them in their own married life, and so they would have to take one another "for better or for worse, for richer or for poorer, in sickness and in health, until death." He then told them to base the security of their wedded life on the principle of self-sacrifice. He then came to this powerful thought:

"Henceforth you belong entirely to each other; you will be one in mind, one in heart, and one in affections. And whatever sacrifices you may hereafter be required to make to preserve this common life, always make them generously. Sacrifice is usually difficult and irksome. Only love can make it easy; and perfect love can make it a joy. We are willing to give in proportion as we love. And when love is perfect, the sacrifice is complete."

The heart of Our Lady's urgent message at Fatima focuses on the conversion of sinners. When the little visionaries Lucia, Francisco, and Jacinta saw the vision of hell during Our Lady's apparition on July 13, 1917 at the Cova da Iria, an indelible reminder was given to them of how urgent it is that the souls of all God's children be saved. The impact of the vision bore great fruit in their lives. All of them, but especially little Jacinta, the youngest of the visionaries, realized how important it was to pray for sinners so that all would be saved in Heaven and none would be lost in Hell. Our Lady confirmed this aspect of her message in her August apparition. At one point toward the end of the apparition Our Lady's face suddenly became sad and she said to the three little children: "Pray, pray very much, and make sacrifices for sinners; for many souls go to hell, because there are none to sacrifice themselves and to pray for them."

The Call To Be Intercessors

Now let us focus on Our Lady's call to prayer as an intercession for sinners. Our Lady emphasized the fact that many souls are lost from God specifically because there is no one to pray for them. If they were praying for themselves, the need for intercessors would be less. But if they are not praying for themselves and they need prayer to obtain God's graces, especially the grace of conversion away from sin and to God, then how will they ever come to the Lord unless someone else does the praying for them? Let us use an example from the Scriptures that can illustrate how important it is for those who are in good spiritual health to help those who are not, to receive God's mercy. Let us take the story of the paralyzed man who was brought to Jesus (Mk 2:1-12). Because the man was physically paralyzed, he obviously could not walk. If he were to get to Jesus for healing, others would have to bring him. That is precisely what four men did for him, carrying him on a mat. When they arrived at the house where Jesus was, they could not enter because of a great crowd that filled the house. They began to tear away the tiles on the roof so that they could lower the man on his mat before Jesus. The Gospel then tells us: "When Jesus saw their faith, he said to the paralytic, 'My son, your sins are forgiven.'" The point of intercession in this important miracle is the fact that just like this paralytic could not have come to Christ on his own because he could not walk, so many people are so steeped in sin in their lives that they are paralyzed in a sense because they cannot turn to the Lord for mercy on their own. Just as the paralytic had to be carried by others, we are called by Our Lady to carry sinners to Christ spiritually by our prayers and sacrifices. This is what the role of spiritual intercession is all about. We also noticed that the Gospel said "When Jesus saw their faith," and not simply the faith of the paralytic, He was moved to work this miracle. In a similar way, Jesus is moved to mercy for sinners when we bring those sinners by our prayers to His feet.

This role of intercession, then, is very important because there are so many people in the world today who never give God a thought in their lives. Many are trapped by our three spiritual enemies: the world, the flesh, and the devil (pride). It is part of our Christian call through Baptism that we be concerned for the physical, but especially the spiritual needs of our brothers and sisters in Christ! This is why Our Lady told the children "Pray, pray very much and make sacrifices for sinners."

The Power of Intercession
Examples in Scripture

All of us, as followers of Jesus, are called to a ministry of intercession. Scripture is filled with examples of how the prayer of intercession turned the hand of God's justice away from punishing His people on various occasions. When the Israelites had sinned in the desert by adoring the idol of the golden calf they had made, God told Moses He would reject His people and raise up for Moses a more faithful people. Here is what God said to Moses: "I see how stiff-necked this people is," continued the Lord to Moses. "Let me alone, then, that my wrath may blaze up against them to consume them. Then I will make of you a great nation" (Ex 32:9-10). Notice that God says to Moses: "Let me alone." It is as if the prayer of intercession by Moses had almost bound up the Lord so that He could not longer destroy His people. This is a very powerful example of intercession. Without Moses' plea on behalf of the people, God's justice would have destroyed them. So even today, our sins offend God so much that were it not for those who intercede for sinners and plead for their conversion, they would have been lost from God for all eternity. Remember, if God had found ten just people living in Sodom and Gomorrah, those cities would have been spared. Their lives, their virtues, and their holiness would have led to the conversion of those living lives displeasing to God. As the Cure of Ars, St. John Vianney once said: "Were it not for a few chaste persons in the world, God would long ago have destroyed the whole world!"

In the New Testament Our Lord himself shows us an example of intercessory prayer when He prayed for Peter to be strengthened so that Peter in turn could strengthen the other Apostles (Lk 22:31-32).

The Example of St. Monica

Perhaps one of the greatest examples of intercessory prayer was that of St. Monica. Her son, Augustine, was living a very immoral life. He had lived with two different women outside of marriage and even had a son by one of them. This crushed the loving and faithful heart of his mother. However, St. Monica did not give in to despair. She knew that the mercy of God endures forever and so she prayed her heart out that God's mercy would touch her son with the grace of conversion. St. Augustine tells us that for sixteen years his mother went morning and evening to pray in the church for his conversion. She prayed so earnestly that the floor where she knelt in prayer was always wet with her tears. This factor made someone say to her: "It is impossible that the son of so many tears could ever be lost." And what a grace of conversion was given. It not only made St. Augustine turn from a life of sin to one of holiness and serving God as one of the greatest bishops and doctors of the Church, but it also made Monica a saint. And there are many modern "Monicas" in the Church today interceding for their children and grandchildren. As we heed Our Lady's call for prayer and sacrifice as intercessors, we too will grow in holiness.

The Example of the Children at Fatima

In the study of spiritual theology, it is evident that the desire for the salvation of souls is a grace that God infuses more powerfully into the hearts of those who grow close to Him. St. Francis of Assisi, for example, used to say that nothing should take precedence to the work of the salvation of souls, for which Jesus shed His Precious Blood. This fact was so true of the lives of the three shepherds of Fatima. They made constant sacrifices, offering everything they could as a sacrifice. And they prayed, especially the Rosary and the prayers of intercession that the Angel of Peace, the Angel of Portugal, had taught them. The Pardon Prayer is a powerful example of the prayer of intercession: "My God, I believe, I adore, I hope and I love You! I beg pardon for those who do not believe, do not adore, do not hope, and do not love You." The children prayed this prayer over and over throughout the day.

One of the most striking examples was that of little Jacinta. A couple of years after the apparitions of Our Lady ended, she had gotten very sick and was very near to death. Our Lady appeared to her and told little Jacinta she would have two choices: Either Our Lady would take her immediately to Heaven or she could stay on earth for six more months to pray for the salvation of souls. Despite how much this very young girl longed to be in Heaven with Jesus and Our Lady, she deferred her eternal happiness and asked to stay on earth so that she could pray for the salvation of sinners. When the Blessed Mother came six months later to prepare to take her to Heaven, she told Jacinta that in the six months she had stayed on earth her prayers and sacrifices had saved 50,000 souls for God!

Are we prepared to become zealous intercessors for the salvation of souls, so that all will be saved and none will be lost?

THE CHRISTIAN MEANING OF SUFFERING IN THE LIGHT OF THE MESSAGE OF FATIMA OUR LADY HAS ASKED FOR REPARATION FOR SINS

In our current series of articles, we have already looked at three things Our Lady has asked for in our spiritual struggle, namely, suffering, sacrifice and intercession (intercessory prayer). In suffering, we try to accept and bear with any painful experiences, physical or spiritual, that God may send us or allow to come our way. By uniting our sufferings to those of Jesus through His Blessed Mother, our sufferings take on a redemptive merit. Sacrifice is a spontaneous offering of anything we feel moved to offer up in honor of the Lord and with the desire to obtain God's mercy for ourselves and others. The Angel of Peace told the three children to make many sacrifices, and to make them of everything they could. Primarily we make sacrifices by denying ourselves things we like. But we can also make sacrifices of anything we do, such as driving to work, shopping, doing homework, washing dishes, or helping a neighbor. Intercession is the offering of our prayers for a specific person or group for any need they may have, but especially to obtain the graces of conversion and God's mercy for those who are not seeking these graces on their own. The Pardon Prayer which the Angel of Peace taught the children is a perfect example of intercessory prayer:

"My God, I believe, I adore, I hope and I love You! I beg pardon for those who do not believe, do not adore, do not hope and do not love You."

Reparation Is Different

Reparation differs from suffering, sacrifice and intercession, but is closely connected to them. These three spiritual works are the means we use to obtain God's graces for ourselves or others. Reparation is really the motive or reason or good we want to obtain by our sufferings, sacrifices and intercessory prayers. In fact, as we shall see, when Our Lady or the Angel of Peace requested sacrifices, suffering and prayers from the three little shepherds, Lucia, Francisco and Jacinta, it was usually mentioned that this was to make reparation to God or to Our Lady for sins by which they have been offended, as well as for the conversion of those who committed these sins.

What Is Reparation?

In general, reparation consists of making amends or atonement for the harm done by sin. We make atonement to God for our sins and those of others by prayer and penance (sacrifice and suffering). When we make reparation for the sins of others, this is called "vicarious satisfaction." It is atonement made for an offense not by the person who committed the offence, but by someone else on their behalf. Reparation is necessary for sins to be forgiven. It was because many sinners are not making reparation for their own sins that Our Lady of Fatima asked for our prayers and penances, to offer up with the merits of Jesus' prayers and sufferings for their conversion and salvation. Remember that Jesus Himself made reparation (vicarious satisfaction) for our sins by His life, death and Resurrection, because none of us by our own merits could ever make adequate reparation for one of our offenses against God, especially any mortal sin.

There is another aspect of reparation that should be mentioned, which shows why it is so important. It can be seen in comparison to restitution for certain sins. If a person steals from another or deliberately harms the good name of another by revealing hidden sins of that person or by making up lies to slander that person, the offender must repent of his sins to be forgiven. But he must also make atonement or reparation for the harm he has done to the person by his sin. The thief must return the stolen property or its equivalent. The bad-mouth must either tell those he spoke to that he was lying, or say good things about the person he defamed. This is part of the act of reparation. When it comes to sins against God (which include offenses against Our Lady or holy persons or sacred things), since He is in Heaven He cannot be directly harmed. However, He has a temporal honor and glory due to Him on earth. When we blaspheme or dishonor God, we have damaged or destroyed, so to speak, God's earthly honor and glory. This must be repaired by acts of reparation. When someone dishonors God and sins against Him, the sinner is saying in effect: "God, I hate You!" When someone makes reparation, they say to God in effect: "God, I love You!" to repair the dishonor due to God's earthly glory. The same holds true for dishonor or blasphemy against the Blessed Virgin Mary.

Finally, when God's honor is offended, the members of the Mystical Body, the Church, are also offended. Spiritual harm can be done to them also, such as scandal, bad example, fear of persecution. Reparation by prayer and penance can heal some of these bad effects and strengthen the faithful. At other times, reparatory actions may be offered – e.g. offering a novena in reparation when a church has been broken into and ransacked.

Reparation in the Message of Fatima

The motive of reparation plays a very important role in the Fatima Message. We find the call to reparation in almost every one of its aspects.

Reparation through Prayer

The Angel of Peace taught the three visionaries the Peace Prayer, meant for the conversion of sinners and reparation from their sins. Likewise, Our Lady in all six of her apparitions to the three children stressed the importance of the Rosary to obtain world peace and the conversion of sinners. In her August apparition, Our Lady stressed the need to pray much and offer sacrifices to prevent souls from going to hell.

Reparation through Sacrifice

The Angel of Peace, in the summer of 1916, introduced the children to the importance of sacrifice as reparation and for conversion of sinners.

"Make of everything you can a sacrifice and offer it to God as an act of reparation for the sins by which He is offended and in supplication for the conversion of sinners…"

As we saw just above, Our Lady also encouraged the children to make sacrifices as reparation. In July, Our Lady taught the children a "Sacrifice Prayer:"

"Sacrifice yourselves for sinners and say many times, especially whenever you make any sacrifice: 'O Jesus, it is for love of You, for the conversion of sinners, and in reparation for the sins committed against the Immaculate Heart of Mary.'"

Reparation through Sufferings

The Angel of Peace, when encouraging the children to make sacrifices of reparation, added: "Above all, accept and bear with submission, the suffering which the Lord will send you." Our Lady, in her first apparition, stressed acceptance of sufferings as a reparation.

"Are you willing to offer yourselves to God and bear all the sufferings He wills to send you, as an act of reparation for the sins by which He is offended, and of supplication for the conversion of sinners?"

The children generously said "yes" and they did suffer:

disbelief (esp. by Lucia's family), ridicule by neighbors and strangers, endless interrogations by church authorities, persecution and threats by the anti-religious authorities, and the like. But their sufferings, united to those of Jesus, helped to save many souls.

Eucharistic Reparation

Reparation to Jesus in the Most Blessed Sacrament plays a major role in the Fatima message. Fatima and the Holy Eucharist were connected from the very beginning when Our Lady appeared on May 13, which was then the Feast of Our Lady of the Most Blessed Sacrament. In his third apparition (Fall 1916), the Angel of Peace, came while the children were kneeling down with their heads to the ground, praying devoutly the Pardon Prayer he had taught them. The angel was holding a chalice in his left hand, with a Eucharistic Host above it. All of a sudden, Host and chalice remained suspended in the air. The angel then knelt next to the children and all had their heads profoundly bowed to the ground in reverent adoration of Jesus in the Blessed Sacrament. He taught them another prayer we call the Angel's Prayer. It focuses on reparation to Jesus for the offenses He receives in the Blessed Sacrament.

"Most Holy Trinity, Father, Son and Holy Spirit, I adore You profoundly. I offer You the most precious Body, Blood, Soul and Divinity of Jesus Christ, present in all the tabernacles of the world, in reparation for the outrages, sacrileges and indifference by which He is offended. By the infinite merits of the Sacred Heart of Jesus and the Immaculate Heart of May, I beg the conversion of poor sinners."

The Angel of Peace then gave the Eucharist as Holy Communion to the children. This apparition and the reception of Holy Communion inspired in the children a deep devotion to Jesus in the Blessed Sacrament. They recited this prayer frequently. It especially made them aware of the offenses Jesus suffers in the Holy Eucharist. They are three: (1) outrages by which the Blessed Sacrament is horribly desecrated and treated with the utmost indignity; (2) sacrileges when Jesus is received in Holy Communion by persons who know they are in mortal sin and are therefore unworthy to receive Jesus; and (3) indifference which could include receiving Holy Communion without proper preparation or an appropriate thanksgiving, or talking, chewing gum or deliberately being distracted in church.

At the close of Our Lady's first apparition, she opened her hands and the children were enveloped in a brilliant light that made them see themselves in God. Then, by an interior impulse, they prayed on their knees: "O Most Holy Trinity, I adore You! My God, my God, I love You in the Most Blessed Sacrament!"

Later on, young Francisco developed a special love and devotion to Jesus in the Blessed Sacrament. Lucia said that when Francisco visited a church, he liked to pray behind the altar at the foot of the tabernacle. He liked to pray hidden to the "hidden Jesus" in the Blessed Sacrament. He offered his severe sufferings and his time in church as reparation to console Our Lord, "because of his great love for Jesus Who was so offended!"

Reparation to the Immaculate Heart of Mary

Like Eucharistic reparation, reparation of Our Lady's

Immaculate Heart has an important part in the Fatima message. As we already saw above, this kind of reparation was included in the "Sacrifice Prayer,"

"O Jesus, it is for love of You, for the conversion of sinners, and in reparation for the sins committed against the Immaculate Heart of Mary."

The three shepherds had seen the sorrowful Heart of Mary during her apparition on June 13, 1917. Her Heart was pierced by a crown of thorns which represented the sins by which Our Lady was offended. Sr. Lucia said in her description of this vision that Our Lady was seeking reparation for these outrages caused by the sins of humanity.

Most significant of all was the reparation related to the devotion of the Five First Saturdays. The Christ Child and Our Lady appeared to Sr. Lucia, who was a postulant with the Sisters of St. Dorothy in Pontevedra, Spain, on December 10, 1925. In the apparition, Our Lady's Heart was surrounded by a crown of piercing thorns. Sr. Lucia described what happened in one of her memoirs:

"...the Christ Child said: 'Have compassion on the Heart of your most holy Mother, covered with thorns, with which ungrateful men pierce it at every moment, and there is no one to make an act of reparation to remove them.' Then the most holy Virgin said: 'Look, my daughter, at my Heart, surrounded with thorns with which ungrateful men pierce me at every moment by their blasphemies and ingratitude. You at least try to console me and say that I promise to assist at the hour of death, with the graces necessary for salvation, all those who, on the first Saturday of five consecutive months, shall confess (their sins), receive Holy Communion, recite five decades of the Rosary, and keep me company for fifteen minutes while meditating on the fifteen mysteries of the Rosary, with the intention of making reparation to me.'"

As we can see, Our Lady enumerated 4 parts to the Five First Saturdays devotion:

1) confession, 2) Holy Communion, 3) a Rosary, and 4) fifteen minutes in heart-to-heart prayer with her. What is important is that all 4 parts are to be done in a spirit of reparation to her Immaculate Heart. How important this devotion is and the reparation it requires can be seen from the fact that Our Lady promised that, along with the consecration of Russia, (which Saint John Paul II did on March 25, 1984, with the overwhelming majority of Bishops of the world), it would lead to the conversion of Russia and of many sinners, to the triumph of her Immaculate Heart and to an era of Peace for the world! We could not hope for more! Let us do our part by reparation!

CHAPTER SIX

MARY, TEACH US TO PRAY
THE PRAYER OF ADORATION

Most Catholics who are baptized as infants are taught their prayers by others as they grow up usually beginning with their parents and grandparents, as well as other special people, such as a favorite aunt or close friend. This has been the case for generation after generation in human history. We may well ask the question then, "Did Our Lady teach Jesus as a Child to pray?" We can only presume she did, since it was the mother's role in Jewish families to be responsible for the earliest religious formation of the children.

Using this as a starting point we can say that Mary has a vital role in teaching all of her spiritual children, even now, to pray. Wouldn't she be the best of teachers? The beginning of a beautiful poem that Ven. Archbishop Sheen loved to quote (written by Mary Dixon Thayer) captures this idea very powerfully:

> Lovely Lady dressed in blue,
> Teach me how to pray!
> God was just your little boy,
> Tell me what to say! ...

Although Sacred Scripture does not tell us a great deal about Mary's prayer life, it does provide enough to teach us about the basics of prayer. We can add to that scriptural evidence some other points on prayer that Our Lady has given in her various apparitions, especially at Fatima.

Purposes of Prayer

Those who write about prayer tell us there are four basic purposes of prayer. In other words we can pray motivated by one or more different concerns. An easy way to remember the four purposes of prayer is to take the word ACTS, and use each letter for a different kind of prayer. A is for adoration or the prayer of praise. C is for contrition or the prayer of expressing sorrow for our sins. T is for the prayer of thanksgiving by which we express our gratitude to God for all that He gives us. S stands for the prayer of supplication. By this we mean the various petitions we offer to God expressing our needs and concerns, or those of others.

Prayer of Adoration

The prayer of adoration is the first form of prayer we owe to God. It acknowledges and expresses God's complete sovereignty and authority over our lives. By its very nature, adoration can only be given to God alone. This adoration due to God is known by the technical Latin word

145

"latria." However, we can give honor to the saints and angels. We honor the Blessed Mother with a special form of honor called "hyperdulia." We offer to the angels and saints an honor called "dulia."

Mary and the Prayer of Adoration

We find expressions of this prayer of adoration in Our Lady's beautiful prayer called the Magnificat (Lk 1:46-55). This prayer expresses the mind and heart of "the poor in spirit" (Mt 5:3) whom Jesus blesses in the Gospel beatitudes. It is often called the "canticle of the poor," because in this beautiful prayer (Magnificat) Mary expresses her complete acknowledgement of God's sovereignty over her life and her complete dependence on Him. Let us see how she expresses this.

God's sovereignty is acknowledged because of three reasons. First, God created us. Only God can make something from nothing. When God created the world and everything in it, He did it by His supreme power and authority and completely out of love. If God did not create us, we would be back where we were before He created us, namely, nothing more than a simple possible thought in the mind of God. But God in His infinite love chose to create us. Therefore, whatever we are and whatever we have comes to us from God's gracious goodness in creating us. This is why St. Paul could ask, "What do you possess that you have not received? But if you have received it, why are you boasting as if you did not receive it?" (1 Cor 4:7). In her canticle Mary acknowledges that everything she has and is has been given to her by God. As she expresses it: "He has looked upon His handmaid in her lowliness...The Mighty One has done great things for me, and holy is His Name..." (Lk 1: 48-49). Mary takes no credit for all the favors given her. She only expresses her great praise of God who has been so good to her. That is why she begins her canticle with the words "My soul proclaims the greatness of the Lord; and my spirit rejoices in God my Savior..." (Lk 1: 46-47).

Mary also acknowledges God's sovereignty by recognizing that it is God Who sustains us by His divine providence and daily care for our lives. She expresses it: "His mercy is from age to age to those who fear Him...the hungry He has filled with good things...He has helped Israel His servant, remembering His mercy" (Lk 1:50, 53-54). Mary recognizes that we depend on God for our very continued existence. He sustains our natural as well as supernatural life by His mercy.

Finally, Mary acknowledges God's sovereignty by recognizing Him as the final destiny of our life. We will all return to God at the end of our earthly journey. He will be our Judge. He will reward us or punish us as our deeds deserve. Mary praises God for this: "For He has looked upon His handmaid's lowliness; behold, from now on all will call me blessed...remembering His mercy according to His promise to our fathers, to Abraham and to his descendants forever" (Lk 1: 48, 54-55).

Learning from Our Lady

Mary's profound sentiments of adoration certainly help us in our practice of the prayer of adoration. As we acknowledge God as our Creator, Provider, and Judge, our faith grows stronger. We are moved spontaneously to acknowledge God's goodness to us and our complete dependence upon Him. This is important today when the faith of so many Catholics seems so weak. Perhaps many

147

have forgotten the basic underlying truths that give rise to the spirit of adoration. People forget that God created them – they did not create themselves. People forget that God is the source of all our goods Who provides what we need for our daily lives – we are not the primary source of all that we need to live by. People forget that we will not live in this world forever – at the end of each of our lives, we will be meeting God as our Judge. Mary reminds us of all these profound truths.

Our words of adoration to God naturally motivate us to love Him and serve Him in our actions, which will praise Him as much as our words. Our Lady offered adoration to God not only by her prayers but even more importantly by her complete obedience to His plan for her life when she responded to the Archangel's message "Behold I am the handmaid of the Lord. May it be done to me according to your word" (Lk 1:38). Imitating Mary, let us give adoration and praise to God both in our words and in our deeds.

Mary, Teach Us to Pray
The Prayer of Contrition

The prayer of contrition or sorrow for our sins is very important for all of us. Because we sin daily by offending God or our neighbor, we need to daily express sorrow for the wrongs we have done. So the prayer of contrition should accompany us every day during our spiritual journey through this life. However, once we reach the Kingdom of Heaven, we will no longer need this prayer. Why not? Because in order to enter Heaven we need to be completely sinless like Mary. Once we pass the "pearly gates," whether directly from this life if we have been holy enough or with a stopover in Purgatory where the final purification from the remains of our sins will be completed, then our repenting days will be over. We will in Heaven simply praise God for His mercy for all eternity. We will no longer have the burden of guilt from our sins. All that will have been removed.

Mary and the Prayer of Contrition

As we said, Mary did not experience the need for the prayer of contrition because she was absolutely sinless throughout her life. Privileged with the gift of her Immaculate Conception, she never knew the stain of Original Sin. At the same time, her soul possessed a "fullness of grace" (cf. Lk 1:28) which would have kept all sin from her will. Furthermore, all through her life her will was constantly in conformity with God's Will. Never once, not even for one moment, was her will in rebellion against what the Lord asked of her. As a result, sin was totally absent from her life. Therefore, she had no need to repent or express sorrow for any sin.

What then can we learn from Our Lady about repentance from sins? Some people might feel she would have nothing to tell us about this because she had never experienced the need to repent. But that would be like saying that a doctor who has never experienced cancer cannot diagnose a condition of cancer in someone and apply the proper remedies. Actually, Our Blessed Lady understood sin far more clearly than any other creature of God. She understood it not by experiencing its malice and the distortions it causes in our own lives, but she knew it in its gravity of offending God. After all, we can only realize the enormous evil of sin when we consider that Jesus, the Son of God become Man, had to suffer and die to atone for all our sins. In this suffering and death Mary was her Son's constant companion, even to the foot of the cross!

Our Lady Loves Sinners

One of the most beautiful titles we give to Our Lady is to call her the "Refuge of Sinners." Don't we constantly invoke her in this role when we pray each Hail Mary? What words of great confidence in her loving compassion we say to her when we pray "Holy Mary, Mother of God, pray for us sinners now and at the hour of our death." Our Lady does not love sin nor does she condone it. At Fatima, for example, she told the young visionaries, "tell the people to not offend The Lord our God anymore, because He is already so much offended!" Though Our Lady hates sin so much since she knows how much it offends God, she has an indescribable love for her children who are sinners in this life.

Our Lady Intercedes for Sinners

One can only imagine how powerful are the prayers of Mary with her Son pleading for the graces of forgiveness and conversion for sinners. If St. Thérèse, the Little Flower, could say that she wanted to spend her eternity doing good on earth as long as the world existed, how much more does this apply to Our Blessed Lady who is constantly concerned about the welfare of her spiritual children! She can never forget the words of her Son Who while hanging on the cross and suffering in agony said to her, "Woman, behold your son!" We will only know in Heaven how many graces of conversion came through her prayers! We will only know on the day of judgment how many people repented of their sins "at the hour of death," because Our Lady recalled their constant petition to her in the Hail Mary!

Our Lady Protects Us from Sin

Not only is Our Lady powerful in obtaining conversions from sin, but she is equally powerful in keeping us from going back to sin. In other words, when we express to

Almighty God our sorrow for our sins and invoke Mary's help to change our lives, we can say she in a sense puts "her mantle of protection" over each one of us and keeps us from many temptations coming from the world, the flesh, or the devil. She helps us to remove from our lives those persons, places, and things that may have been occasions of sin in the past. Furthermore, she helps us overcome sinful habits which may have enslaved us to evil. It may take a long and intense struggle to break these habits of sin, but with Mary's help our sorrow will deepen and our desire for real amendment of our lives will become more firm and effective.

Mary's Holiness Challenges Us

The closer we come to Almighty God, the more we realize our own sinfulness and selfishness. It is like a person coming out of darkness toward a tremendous light. In that light they will see themselves more clearly, especially those areas of their lives which they have not given over to God. This will move them to be even more desirous of removing the remnants of selfishness from their hearts. This author once heard about a group of people, most of whom had already been to Confession, who visited a very holy Marian shrine and were overcome with a profound sense of Our Lady's presence. As a result of experiencing her presence so powerfully, they actually had to go to Confession again. In the light of Mary's holiness, their sins became more obvious. We might say, you can only tell how deep the darkness is in contrast to the brilliance of the light. Mary is a light with Christ, her Son, Who is the very Light of the world (cf. Jn 8:12).

Mary Encourages Prayer for the Conversion of Sinners

Our Lady assists us to grow in the prayer of contrition not only by repenting of our own personal sins but also praying for the grace of repentance for our brothers and sisters in Christ whose lives are still caught up in grave sin. This has been an almost constant theme in all of Our Lady's great apparitions, but especially at Fatima. This was obvious after the children had seen hell in the apparition on July 13, 1917, for Our Lady said to them: "You have seen hell where the souls of poor sinners go. To save them (from hell) God wishes to establish in the world devotion to my Immaculate Heart." She even taught us a little prayer to say at the end of each decade of the Rosary: "Oh my Jesus, forgive us our sins, save us from the fires of hell, lead all souls to Heaven, especially those most in need of Your mercy."

One of the fruits of the prayer of contrition is to make us more zealous in wanting to work for the salvation of souls. As St. Padre Pio used to say: "That none may be lost and all may be saved!" When we are genuinely sorry for our own sins, which is what the prayer of contrition is all about, we must of necessity pray that others will experience God's mercy for their sins as well. We will probably not know until we come to Heaven all those on earth whose prayers assisted us in being sorry for our own sins and obtained for us the grace of conversion. But we can be sure that there was one person praying for us and that is our Mother in Heaven. Fittingly do we call her the "Mother of Mercy."

In America every year we celebrate a civil holiday called Thanksgiving Day. It is a day in which as a nation we acknowledge God as the giver of all our gifts and blessings, and so we render Him thanks. It was begun as an American tradition by one of the first groups of settlers, the Pilgrims. After enduring the hardship of their first winter and then planting their crops for the first time, they rejoiced in the harvest. It was then that they celebrated by giving thanks to God.

The underlying sentiment of all thanksgiving is a heartfelt gratitude to God for His goodness and the many blessings He bestows upon His people. We express gratitude for the fact that He created us, that He sustains us and cares for us during our lifetime and that He has destined us to share His eternal happiness in the Kingdom of Heaven.

Gratitude is an absolutely essential quality in our lives for we never want to take the blessings of God for granted. We see in the evidence of Scripture, in the lives of both Jesus and Mary, that a sense of gratitude filled their own prayers. We, in turn, should echo in our own prayers that same attitude of thanksgiving to God for His blessings. Our motivation should be that we recognize God as all good and deserving of all our love.

Jesus and the Prayer of Thanksgiving

When Jesus prayed to His Heavenly Father, He frequently expressed the sentiment of gratitude and thanksgiving for the blessings His Father had bestowed or was about to bestow. Let us look at a few examples. When Jesus was about to multiply the loaves and the fishes, we read: "Jesus then took the loaves of bread, gave thanks, and passed them around to those reclining there; He did the same with the dried fish, as much as they wanted" (Jn 6:11). Another example occurred just before Jesus raised His friend Lazarus from the dead. He prayed to His Heavenly Father: "Father, I thank you for having heard Me. I know that You always hear me; but I have said this, for the sake of the crowd that they may believe that You sent me" (Jn 11:41-42).

Even more so does Jesus give thanks when He institutes the Eucharist at the Last Supper. What more precious gift could there be than the very Body and Blood, Soul and Divinity of Jesus Christ contained for us under the simple signs of bread and wine! The Eucharist was the Father's gift to His people in sending His Divine Son into the world. As Jesus declared: "I myself am the Living

155

Bread come down from Heaven" (Jn 6:51). He had told His Jewish listeners that day, "My Father gives you the true Bread from Heaven" (Jn 6:32). Therefore, as Jesus was ready to give us this unspeakable gift of His Eucharistic Body and Blood, He acknowledges that it is the Father who is giving this true Bread from Heaven to His children. And so we read: "And when He had taken some bread and given thanks, He broke it and gave it to them, saying, 'This is My Body to be given for you. Do this as a remembrance of Me'" (Lk 22:19). Then when He took the cup of wine, He again expressed gratitude to the Father for the beautiful gift He was about to offer in giving His Precious Blood to the disciples: "He likewise took a cup, gave thanks and passed it to them, and they all drank from it. He said to them: 'This is My blood, the blood of the covenant, to be poured out on behalf of many'" (Mk 14:23-24). It is because Jesus gave thanks to His Heavenly Father before giving us His Body and Blood that we call this Sacrament the "Eucharist" from the Greek word meaning "to give thanks."

Another example of thanksgiving in Our Lord's prayers is a reference to the hymn that was sung at the end of the Passover Meal. St. Mark makes reference to this hymn which contains Psalms 114-118. "After singing songs of praise, they walked out to the Mount of Olives" (Mk 14:26). These psalms were basically thanksgiving songs that were used at the conclusion of the Passover celebration. Incidentally, as Ven. Archbishop Fulton Sheen used to observe, that this is the only time it is recorded in the Scriptures that Jesus sang. Ironically, He sang on His way to death!

Mary and the Prayer of Thanksgiving

The heart of the Blessed Mother closely resonated with the heart of Christ her Son. So if Jesus prayed with the sentiments of gratitude and thanksgiving, we would naturally assume that Mary had these same sentiments in her own prayers. We have Mary's most beautiful prayer, The Magnificat, as an example of the sentiments that filled her when she prayed. Although Our Lady does not use the word thanks directly in her canticle, she expresses sentiments that had to be inspired by God's goodness to her. For example, she prays, "For (God) has looked upon His servant in her lowliness; behold from now on all ages shall call me blessed" (Lk 1:48). No doubt Our Lady in her humility is grateful for God choosing her. Furthermore, what He has done for her will so exalt her that all ages to come will acknowledge her as blessed! Again we read "God who is mighty has done great things for me, holy is His name" (Lk 1:49). Mary takes no credit for what has happened to her. Rather, she humbly acknowledges that it was God working in her that has brought about marvels of grace for which all mankind will bless His holy name. A final example of Mary's sentiment of gratitude is expressed in her words: "His mercy is from age to age to those who fear Him" (Lk 1:50). God's mercy is His enduring and compassionate love for His people. He never withdraws that love but continues to give it "from age to age." What we need to do is fear Him. This is not the fear of slaves toward their master or the fear of being punished for some wrong. That fear, called "servile fear," can be useful to get many people to change from a life of sin to the pathway that leads to Heaven. Servile fear might be based on the fact that we fear the loss of Heaven or the pains of Hell. But the fear Our Lady speaks about is the sanctifying gift of the Holy

Spirit. It is called "fear of the Lord." Unlike servile fear which makes us afraid that God may punish us, fear of the Lord makes us afraid that we will disappoint God, that we will not be pleasing to Him or do what He asks of us. Anyone who possesses this fear of the Lord realizes that the worst thing they could ever do is to offend God because He has been so good to them. It would be a deep ingratitude to displease God who has been so lavish in all His blessings. Therefore, the fear of the Lord makes us desire to do everything we can to please God. Finally, fear of the Lord instills in the heart a profound realization that the worst tragedy that could ever possibly happen to us is to be separated from God by sin. It makes us cry out in prayer, "Lord, let me never be separated from You!"

Our Own Prayer of Thanksgiving
God Expects Thanksgiving

In imitating Our Lord and Our Blessed Lady, our prayers should have an underlying attitude of thanksgiving. God expects us to express appreciation for His many gifts and blessings. We see this clearly in the incident when Jesus healed ten lepers. When the lepers had asked Jesus to heal them, He sent them off to the priests who had to declare them cleansed of their leprosy. As they went on their way, they were all cleansed. At this point we read in the Gospel story: "Now one of them, realizing that he had been cured, came back praising God in a loud voice. He threw himself on his face at the feet of Jesus and spoke his praises. This man was a Samaritan." Then Jesus said, "Were not all ten made whole? Where are the other nine? Was there no one to return and give thanks to God, except this foreigner?" He said to the man, "Stand up and go your way; your faith has been your salvation" (Lk 17:15-19). Our Lord obviously expected that all ten would have returned to give thanks to God. But only one returned, and ironically he was a Samaritan who in the eyes of the Jewish people at the time would have been considered a heretic and not a true believer. But he had gratitude and expressed it in a beautiful prayer of thanksgiving.

We Need to Give Our Thanks

The Lord healed all ten of the lepers but only one returned. We have to conclude then that Our Lord got only a ten percent return for the investment of His blessings! Many times this is the case even today. How often we easily take God's blessings for granted! How many times do we ask Him to give us all the things we think will make us happy, or all the things we need in times of adversity? But do we remember to go back like the Samaritan leper to say "thanks, Lord for Your goodness!"

At Holy Mass the celebrant has a little dialogue with the People of God before he begins to pray the Eucharistic Prayer. One of the sentiments he expresses is: "Let us give thanks to the Lord our God." And the people respond: "It is right to give Him thanks and praise." This sentiment of thanksgiving genuinely expresses the attitude of the Church in praising Almighty God for His goodness and mercy. A little example of this sense of gratitude is found in the life of the first canonized saint of the Capuchin-Franciscan Order. His name is St. Felix of Cantalice. Whenever he received an alms either for distribution to the poor or for the support of the friars he would always say in Latin "Deo Gratias." This is a phrase that meant "thanks be to God!" He said it so often, that the people nicknamed him Brother Deo Gratias! Wouldn't it be great if we also were characterized by some gratefulness and thanksgiving to God. It would help us never to take the blessings of God for granted.

One of the first things good parents teach their children is that when they receive a gift from someone to say "thank you." This attitude of gratitude should be instinctive in our hearts especially when God is the giver. As we have seen, even Jesus did that when giving us gifts that He knew were coming to us from His Heavenly Father. We also saw Our Lady's example of gratitude for all that God had done in her life. Let us be true children of our Heavenly Father, imitating Christ and the example that Our Lady gives us. Since it was the role of the mother in a Jewish family to raise the children in the teachings of the faith and in prayer, we can almost assume that it was Our Lady who taught Jesus to offer the prayer of thanksgiving. Let us ask Our Lady to teach us the same prayer! After all, every day should be a "thanksgiving day" for anyone who loves the Lord and His Holy Mother.

Mary, Teach Us to Pray
The Prayer of Petition and Intercession

"Father, say a prayer for me!" "Sister, please pray for me!" Probably every Catholic priest and religious has heard these words countless times. Sometimes people just make a general prayer request: "Please pray for me!" At other times, they have very specific intentions. Whatever the need, people are sure to ask for prayers of petition because they are convinced of their power. After all, Our Lord assures us: "Ask and you will receive; seek and you will find; knock and the door will be opened to you. For everyone who asks, receives; and the one who seeks, finds; and to the one who knocks, the door will be opened" (Lk 11:9-10). This is especially true of the power of intercessory prayer.

Jesus and Mary Prayed for Others
Jesus Interceded for the Needs of Others

In His humanity, Jesus is our High Priest before the Father. This means that He is a mediator between the Father and all of mankind. Part of His role is to intercede for us in prayer with His Heavenly Father. He presents our needs to the Father and pleads for mercy for our sins. The most outstanding example of Jesus interceding for the Father's mercy came when He prayed upon the cross, "Father, forgive them, they know not what they do" (Lk 23:34). He pleaded for mercy, not only for those who were actually carrying out His crucifixion, but also for all of us because He was dying to take away all of our sins. They were the real cause of His death. We must imitate this powerful example of Our Lord and be ready to pray even for those who cause us harm in some way.

Another powerful example of Jesus' intercessory prayer occurred during the Last Supper when Jesus said to Peter: "Simon, behold Satan has demanded to sift all of you like wheat, but I have prayed that your own faith may not fail; and once you have turned back, you must strengthen your brothers" (Lk 22:31-32). The Lord prayed for strength for Peter both for himself and as an instrument of strength for the other Apostles. Do we ever imitate this prayer by praying for others in their special needs? If our love is to grow, it is necessary to expand the focus of our prayers to include the concerns we have for those who are in trial and tribulation.

Our Blessed Lady Intercedes As Well

Our Lady was no doubt the closest imitator of Jesus. As He prayed for others, we find evidence of Mary bringing

162

the needs of others to her Divine Son. For example, at the wedding feast of Cana Our Lady makes known to Jesus the needs of the young couple whose wedding celebration they were attending. Her prayer of concern was simple yet powerful, "They have no wine" (Jn 2:3). Our Lady's concern was for the young couple not to be embarrassed by a lack of wine for their guests. This would probably have forced them to cut short their week-long wedding celebration. She was not asked to do something; she spontaneously saw the need and offered her words of intercession. They must have been very powerful because they moved Jesus to work His first miracle. In our own lives, let us imitate Mary's spirit of spontaneously interceding for those who are in genuine need.

We see Our Lady again in an intercessory role springing from her spiritual motherhood of the Church. She was surrounded by the apostles and that first band of Jesus' disciples gathered together in the Upper Room in Jerusalem for nine days prior to the great feast of Pentecost. They were awaiting the promised gift of the Holy Spirit. "All these devoted themselves with one accord to prayer, together with some women, and Mary the mother of Jesus, and His brothers" (Acts 1:14). Mary is joining her prayers to those of the first members of the Church praying for the gift of the Holy Spirit to come. How powerful her intercession must have been! After all, when the Holy Spirit came upon her at Nazareth, she conceived the Second Divine Person of the Blessed Trinity as man within her womb. This was the greatest event in human history. Our prayers of intercession should imitate Mary's example in praying for the needs of our brothers and sisters and in a special way for the many needs of the Church in our time. Do we pray for vocations? Or for our brothers and sisters in Christ who are persecuted? Or for the message of the Gospel to be spread by zealous missionaries in our time?

Our Lady Requests Our Intercessory Prayer

Not only did Our Lady practice intercessory prayer in her own lifetime but in her apparitions she has encouraged her spiritual children to offer constant intercessory prayer. This is especially true of her message at Fatima.

What did Our Lady ask us to pray for? First and most importantly she asked for prayers and sacrifices for the conversion of sinners. She told the visionaries: "Many souls go to hell, because there are none to sacrifice themselves and to pray for them." There is no greater intention that we can have nor any greater work of mercy that we could carry out than to pray and sacrifice for the eternal salvation of all those for whom Jesus endured His agony, shed His blood and died on the cross. St. Francis of Assisi used to say: "Let nothing take precedence to the work of salvation of souls for whom Christ died." In our world today filled with immorality and an absence of God, we need prayer to obtain God's grace to renew faith, hope and love in the hearts of people in our secularized society.

A second reason Our Lady asked us to pray was for peace in the world. Our Lady warned that war and other forms of suffering would come if we continued to offend Almighty God. She told the children, tell the people: "Do not offend the Lord our God any more, because He is already so much offended." Today more than ever in our secular society we need the power of prayer as well as sacrifice to change the morality of people. The widespread effects of the Culture of Death, namely, abortion, euthanasia, embryonic stem cell research, and assisted suicide, all manifest the urgent need for the conversion of hearts and the changing of the values of our culture. We need to bring the power of the Gospel to bear once again on the human race. We have lost the sense of the "sanctity of life" from conception to natural death. Only God can restore it, and we can best obtain that when we pray earnestly and offer sacrifices for that intention. At the same time, we must defend the dignity of the family as God created it, namely, one man married to one woman. Same-sex marriage and homosexual lifestyle are contrary to God's law. We need, by prayer, to support God's plan for the dignity and purpose of the family which is mutual love of husband and wife and the begetting and upbringing of children.

Our Lady of Fatima had told the children that World War I, then raging, would end. She said an era of peace would be given to the people if they heeded her message. However, if they did not, she said another and more terrible war would begin. Unfortunately, we know that as World War II. We must, by prayer and penance, transform the world to prevent it from heading on a path of total self-destruction.

The Rosary – A Powerful Prayer of Petition

The prayer that Our Lady asked for in all of her apparitions at Fatima was the Rosary. She said it was powerful enough to end wars, to bring world peace, and to convert sinners. Let us imitate Mary's intercessory prayer by carrying out her message and plan for world peace. There is an absolute urgency that we do this. Our Blessed Mother has told us what we need to do! Now we simply have to carry out her request. It was for this reason that our Holy Father, Pope Emeritus Benedict XVI said: "Learn the message of Fatima! Live the message of Fatima! Spread the message of Fatima!"

CHAPTER SEVEN

THE FIVE FIRST SATURDAYS DEVOTION
A TREASURE FROM FATIMA

One of the most important aspects of Our Lady of Fatima's Message was her request for the devotion we call the "Five First Saturdays." I remember as a young boy how many people made this devotion in honor of Our Lady on the First Saturday of five consecutive months. It seemed to be the natural complement to the Nine First Fridays' devotion in honor of the Sacred Heart of Jesus.

Our Lord Himself had requested the First Friday devotion at the time of His apparitions to St. Margaret Mary Alacoque in the Visitation Monastery in Paray-le-Monial in France, during which He revealed the overwhelming love of His Sacred Heart for all of us. It was a devotion of prayer and reparation for those who offend His infinite love either by hatred, neglect or indifference.

The Five First Saturdays devotion is also meant to be a devotion of prayer and reparation for those who offend against the Immaculate Heart of Our Lady. When I practiced this devotion as a young boy (and I still practice it today), I did not realize its beauty and depth. It was only years later that I learned that each of the Five First Saturdays was to be offered in reparation for very specific offenses against the Immaculate Heart of Our Lady. I wonder today how many Catholics even know of the devotion of the Five First Saturdays because it does not seem to be widely encouraged. Furthermore, I wonder how many of the people who do practice this devotion actually realize its beauty and depth. In this article, I would like to share the historical background of this devotion. In subsequent articles, I will offer reflections on the meaning of the reparation called for in each of the Five First Saturdays.

Our Lady Reveals Her Intention at Fatima

When our Blessed Mother appeared to Lucia, Francisco and Jacinta on July 13, 1917, she confided the main part of her Message to the children. They saw a most frightening vision of Hell, where there were both demons and lost souls in terrifying torment and despair. The young visionaries were completely shaken by the vision. Then Our Lady spoke kindly but sadly to them: "You have

168

seen Hell where the souls of poor sinners go. To save them, God wishes to establish in the world devotion to my Immaculate Heart. If what I say to you is done, many souls will be saved and there will be peace" (Lucia's 4th Memoir). Our Lady's Message was focused on the salvation of souls and specifically on her Immaculate Heart as God's chosen instrument to bring this about.

As Our Lady continued speaking, she revealed to the children that World War I, then raging, would come to an end. But she warned that a worse war, along with famine and persecution of the Church, especially of the Holy Father, would come about if people did not cease offending God. Then she added in her great maternal love for us: "To prevent this, I shall come to ask for the consecration of Russia to my Immaculate Heart and the Communion of Reparation on the First Saturdays. If my requests are heeded, Russia will be converted and there will be peace; if not, she will spread her errors throughout the world, causing wars and persecutions of the Church. The good will be martyred, the Holy Father will have much to suffer, various nations will be annihilated..." We have seen all of these unfortunate evils occur in the world in the 20th century.

Our Lady did add, however, a message of hope when she said, "In the end, my Immaculate Heart will triumph. The Holy Father will consecrate Russia to me, and she will be converted, and a period of peace will be granted to the world." Ever since Saint John Paul II made the Collegial Consecration requested by Our Lady of Fatima on March 25, 1984, we have begun to see the conversion of Russia back to God and now await "a period of peace" to come upon the world. But more must be done, and this is where the devotion of the Five First Saturdays plays a vital role.

Our Lady Keeps Her Promise

Our Lady had said to the young visionaries, "I will come (again) to ask for...the Communion of Reparation on the First Saturdays..." Our Lady kept her promise on December 10, 1925. Francisco and Jacinta had already been taken to Heaven. Lucia, the remaining visionary of Fatima, was a postulant for the Dorothean Sisters at a convent in Pontevedra, Spain. Our Lady appeared to Lucia together with the Child Jesus. He spoke first to Lucia: "Have compassion on the Heart of your Most Holy Mother, which is covered with thorns that ungrateful men drive into it every instant, while there is no one who does an act of reparation to withdraw them for her." We know that all sin ultimately offends God. So every act of reparation is ultimately directed to Him, to restore His earthly honor and glory that sin has offended and diminished. However, here Our Lord Himself extends the spirit of reparation to restore the honor of the Immaculate Heart of His Blessed Mother that sins directly against her have diminished. How powerful are the words of His own request: "Have compassion on the Heart of your Most Holy Mother!"

Then Our Lady, showing her Heart to Lucia, spoke, announcing her request: "Look, my daughter, at my Heart encircled with thorns, with which ungrateful men wound it every moment by their blasphemies and ingratitude. You, at least try to console me and say that I promise to assist at the hour of death, with the graces necessary for salvation, all who on the first Saturday of five consecutive months confess, receive Holy Communion, recite five decades of the Rosary, and keep me company with the purpose of making reparation to me."

What a magnificent promise of Our Lady: that she would assist us with the graces needed for salvation in the most important moment of our lives — the time of our death! Do we not pray to her for this every time we pray the Hail Mary: "Holy Mary, Mother of God, pray for us sinners, now and at the hour of our death?"

Our Lady states, then, what is required to obtain her promise by practicing the First Saturdays devotion. We can summarize these requirements into six points: (1) go to Confession (usually within the week before or after the First Saturday), (2) receive Holy Communion on the First Saturday itself, (3) recite five decades of the Rosary, (4) meditate on one or more of the Mysteries of the Rosary for an additional 15 minutes, (5) do all of these things with the intention of making reparation to the Immaculate Heart of Mary, and (6) do these things on the First Saturday of five consecutive months.

To complete our understanding of the devotion of reparation on the Five First Saturdays, it is important to know why there are five kinds of reparation, and what each reparation is for. Sister Lucia provided this information for us in a letter dated June 12, 1930. In it she tells us that Our Lord appeared to her in the convent chapel on the night of May 29-30, 1930, and revealed to her the meaning of the five Saturdays. Sister Lucia quotes Our Lord's words to her:

"My daughter, the motive is simple: there are five ways in which people offend and blaspheme against the Immaculate Heart of Mary. There are blasphemies: (1) Against her Immaculate Conception, (2) Against her Virginity, (3) Against her Divine Maternity, refusing at the same time to accept her as the Mother of all mankind,

(4) By those who try publicly to implant in the hearts of children indifference, contempt and even hate against this Immaculate Mother, and (5) By those who insult her directly in her sacred images."

It is obvious from all of the above how important this devotion really is. In the following pages, I would like to reflect on each of the five reasons why Our Lord wants this reparation paid to the Immaculate Heart of His Blessed Mother and ours, too!

"I am the Immaculate Conception!" That is the way the Blessed Virgin Mary identified herself at Lourdes to Saint Bernadette when the saint had asked who she was. What a marvelous description, one that brings great joy to all who love Our Lady. She is, as a Protestant writer once put it, "our tainted human nature's solitary boast!"

The Immaculate Conception of the Blessed Virgin Mary is especially dear to devout Catholics. It declares the belief of the Church, now a defined dogma of the Catholic Faith, that Our Lady, through a special grace and privilege of Almighty God, in view of her becoming the Mother of God, was preserved free from Original Sin and given a fullness of grace from the first moment of her conception.

This privilege of Our Lady is one of the most cherished of Catholic beliefs. It is also one of the most important. Why? Because it shows Jesus' complete power and victory over sin. Jesus came to save us from our sins. He said, "The Son of Man has come to search out and save what was lost" (Lk 19:10). He does this in various ways. In Baptism, He takes away the guilt of Original Sin (and of any personal sins that someone over the age of reason may have committed), while at the same time infusing into that soul a share in His own divine life that He merited for us by His redemptive death. In the Sacrament of Penance, Jesus takes away our personal sins committed after Baptism through the power to forgive sins which He gave to His Apostles on Easter night (cf. Jn 20:22-23), and which has been passed down over the centuries to His bishops and priests.

Now in both of these cases, sin has already affected the person, leaving traces of wounds and weaknesses in its wake, even after they have been forgiven! In the case of Our Lady, her privilege was so great that Original Sin (and consequently personal sin as well) never touched her soul. Hers was an extraordinary form of Redemption: she was redeemed by being preserved from Original Sin in view of the foreseen merits of Jesus, her Divine Son! At the same time, she was filled with such an extraordinary fullness of Sanctifying Grace that some saints believed it surpassed the combined holiness of all the angels and saints together!

"Immaculate Conception" Blasphemed

This blasphemy, no doubt, comes ultimately from Satan himself. The devil inspires it for many reasons. First, he is angry at Jesus' power and victory which this dogma represents. He knows that at the end of time, any power God allows him to have to tempt us will cease completely. He foresees this conquest of Christ over him and his legions in Our Lady's complete victory of sinlessness all through her life from the first moment of her conception. He deeply resents Our Lady's immaculate holiness. It meant that he did not have, even for one instant, any power or influence over her. Our Lady was like a bright light shining through the darkness of Satan's control and deceit. Satan was helpless to block that light, to stop it, to prevent it from showing the evil he intended to inflict on all mankind. Therefore, he inspires anyone, whether they be among his conscious followers in the occult or simply people who are very weak morally, to express hate, ridicule and contempt against Our Lady's marvelous privilege.

The "Woman" Who Crushes the Head of Satan

Another reason the devil hates the privilege of Our Lady's Immaculate Conception is because he sees the Virgin Mary in a special way under this title as the "Woman" who will crush his head! Immediately after Satan deceived our first parents into committing the Original Sin, God said to him, "I will put enmity between you and the woman, and between your offspring and hers; He will crush your head, while you strike at His heel!" (Gen 3:15). When God spoke of the "Woman," He was obviously not referring to Eve of old to crush Satan's head, since she had just personally sinned by pride (wanting to

175

be as a god) and disobedience (eating the forbidden fruit) at his deception.

Who, then, is the "Woman"? The Church sees this as a reference to Mary, the Mother of Jesus and our Mother, too! Jesus Himself twice refers to His own Mother as "Woman." (When I was studying Sacred Scripture in the seminary, they taught us that Jesus' reference to His own Mother as "Woman" was an absolutely unique usage among all ancient Hebrew and Greek literature). The first usage occurs at the wedding feast of Cana (cf. Jn 2:1-11), when Jesus says to His Mother, "Woman, how does this concern of yours involve Me? My hour has not yet come." Moved by the confident trust of His Mother, Jesus then works His first miracle by changing water into wine, thus also inspiring His disciples to believe in Him. The second usage occurs at the cross on Calvary (cf. Jn 19:25-27), when Jesus gives His Mother the care of all His followers represented by John, the "beloved disciple," saying to her, "Woman, behold your son!"

God's words to Satan in Genesis 3:15 are often cited as a "proof text" to support the fact that the dogma of the Immaculate Conception was revealed by God in Sacred Scripture. How is this so? The words we want to focus on are: "I will put enmity between you (the serpent, Satan) and the Woman (Our Lady, the New Eve)." The key word here is "enmity." Enmity means a very bitter hatred. Now, despite how strong our English word enmity is, it cannot convey the full force and intense meaning of the original Hebrew word. The Hebrew root of this word implies such a bitter mutual repulsion between the two, that not for even the briefest moment could they tolerate being in each other's presence. Therefore, Our Lady and Satan would not want to be near each other! So how could Satan have had an influence over the soul of Our Lady, even for one moment? And without such influence or control, the Immaculate Conception represented the beginning of the destruction of Satan's universal influence over sinful mankind. It was, to use God's words, the beginning of the crushing of his head!

Our Lady's Divine Maternity

The Immaculate Conception was a marvelous gift from Our Heavenly Father to the Virgin Mary in view of preparing her to become the Mother of His own Divine Son. This privilege separated Our Lady from any direct personal contact with sin. She was, as a result, sinless and grace-filled! At the moment the Incarnation occurred during the Annunciation, Jesus took His very Flesh and Blood from the absolutely pure body united to the immaculate soul of the Blessed Virgin Mary! In view of this wondrous event, Satan's fury no doubt knew no limits (cf. Rev 12:12). This is an added reason why he has been relentless in stirring up blasphemy and contempt among his followers against this special privilege of Our Lady!

Importance for Reparation

Reparation in this instance is directed at restoring the honor due to Our Lady for God's great privilege to her in view of her becoming the Mother of God. Blasphemy has seriously offended God by dishonoring the extraordinary grace He gave her in her Immaculate Conception. Our reparation atones for this grave dishonor, while praising and venerating the Virgin Mary with appropriate devotion. While carrying Jesus physically in her womb, Our Lady said in her Magnificat: "God who is mighty has done great things for me, and holy is His name" (Lk 1:49).

Besides offering the first of the Five First Saturdays' devotion in reparation for the blasphemies against the Immaculate Conception, a person may choose to wear the Miraculous Medal that was entrusted to Saint Catherine Labouré. Since its design was revealed to the saint in a vision, we must truly say it was formed in Heaven. It bore the significant prayer to Our Lady, "O Mary conceived without sin, pray for us who have recourse to thee." Besides wearing the Miraculous Medal, we should repeat that prayer often, thus making added reparation for blasphemies against the Immaculate Conception. Finally, we should encourage others to practice the Five First Saturdays devotion, and to honor the privilege of Our Lady's Immaculate Conception, thus making further reparation for the blasphemies she has endured. All of this will obtain the special powerful protection of Our Lady against sin and Satan's power in our lives.

THE FIVE FIRST SATURDAYS DEVOTION
REPARATION FOR BLASPHEMIES
AGAINST MARY'S PERPETUAL VIRGINITY

To explain the reason why Our Lady requested Five First Saturdays of reparation, Our Lord said in a vision to Sister Lucia: "... there are five ways in which people offend and blaspheme against the Immaculate Heart of Mary."

One of the most popular titles of Our Blessed Lady is to call her the "Virgin Mary." This is very fitting because it is rooted in Sacred Scripture. When Saint Luke described the Annunciation event, he twice referred to Our Lady as "virgin." "In the sixth month, the angel Gabriel was sent from God to a town of Galilee named Nazareth, to a virgin betrothed to a man named Joseph, of the house of David. The virgin's name was Mary" (Lk 1:26-27). Saint Matthew, in his Gospel account, also stresses Our

Lady's virginity, emphasizing that the conception of Jesus occurred without Our Lady having marital relations with Saint Joseph. "Now this is how the birth of Jesus Christ came about. When His mother Mary was engaged to Joseph, but before they lived together, she was found with child through the power of the Holy Spirit. Joseph her husband, an upright man unwilling to expose her to the law, decided to divorce her quietly. Such was his intention when suddenly the angel of the Lord appeared in a dream and said to him: 'Joseph, son of David, have no fear about taking Mary as your wife. It is by the Holy Spirit that she has conceived this child. She is to have a son and you are to name Him Jesus because He will save His people from their sins.' All this happened to fulfill what the Lord had said through the prophet: 'The virgin shall be with child and give birth to a son, and they shall call Him Emmanuel' (Is 7:14), a name which means 'God is with us.' When Joseph awoke he did as the angel of the Lord had directed him and received her into his home. He had no relations with her at any time before she bore a son, whom he named Jesus" (Mt 1:18-25).

Our Lady's Virginity Was Perpetual

These two Gospel passages clearly state that Our Lady was truly a virgin at the moment she conceived Christ within her womb by the power of the Holy Spirit. In fact, Our Lady's virginity was to be perpetual. This is a dogma of the Catholic Church. Saint Clement of Alexandria (D. 215 A.D.) was one of the earliest Fathers of the Church to express this fact: "O great mystery! Mary, an incorrupt virgin conceived, after conception she brought forth as a virgin, after childbirth she remained a virgin." The First Lateran Council (649 A.D.) under Pope Saint Martin I, later defined Our Lady's perpetual virginity when
180

it condemned anyone who did not acknowledge with the Fathers of the Church that "the holy and ever virgin and immaculate Mary as really and truly the Mother of God, inasmuch as she, in the fullness of time, and without seed, conceived by the Holy Spirit God the Word Himself. Who before all time was born of God the Father, and without loss of integrity brought Him forth, and after His birth preserved her virginity inviolate."

This dogma was traditionally expressed in the formula that Mary was virgin "before, during and after the birth" of Jesus. We have already seen how the meaning of the phrase, "before the birth" of Jesus is clear from Gospel accounts above. Let us look briefly at the other two phrases.

"During the birth" of Jesus grew out of the understanding of the Church, enlightened by the Holy Spirit. It expresses the belief that at the moment of her giving birth to Jesus, through a special divine action, Mary did not lose the physical signs of her virginity. The Fathers of the Church would say that the womb of the Blessed Mother remained closed and intact, and that Jesus passed through the enclosure of her womb much as he passed through the walls of the room where the Apostles were gathered on Easter night with the doors bolted closed (cf. Jn 20: 19).

"After the birth" of Jesus requires a somewhat longer explanation because certain objections have been raised against it over the centuries. This phrase refers to the dogmatic belief in Catholic tradition that Our Lady never had marital relations with Saint Joseph even after the birth of Jesus, but preserved her virginity intact for the rest of her life. Our Lady, as we shall see, was quite concerned to preserve her virginity before conceiving Jesus, so why should we assume she would surrender her virginity afterwards?

Let us look very briefly at the source of the major objections we find here. The biggest difficulty, raised from early Christian centuries, is that Sacred Scripture speaks of Jesus' "brothers" (cf. Mt 13:055; Mk 3:31-35; Mk 6:3). How could Our Lady have remained a perpetual virgin if she had other sons after the birth of Jesus? One explanation given by Saint Epiphanius (c. 403 A.D.) was that the "brothers of the Lord" were really sons of Saint Joseph by a prior marriage, but there is no evidence at all in the Gospels to support this idea. Another and better explanation is the fact that neither Hebrew nor Aramaic, Our Lord's spoken language, had a specific word for "cousin." The word brother was commonly used to indicate actual cousins. (Even today the word brother is used broadly in certain ethnic groups to include simple companions, or in my own case as a Franciscan friar, to include my fellow religious. Now in neither case is there any blood relationship, but simply a fraternal bond.) Furthermore, these "brothers of the Lord" are never called the children of Mary, and in fact two of them, James and Joseph (cf. Mt 13:55: called James and Joses in Mk 6:3), are explicitly said to be the children of another Mary who is certainly not Our Lady (cf. Mt 27:56). One final observation is that elsewhere in the New Testament, the word "brother" is used in a general way to indicate a fellow disciple, not a blood relative (cf. Acts 1:15; 1 Cor 5:11, 15:6).

Mary's Vow of Perpetual Virginity

Our Lady's intention to remain a virgin can be seen in her response to the angel Gabriel's message that she was to become a mother: "How can this be since I do not know man?" (Lk 1:34). Catholic tradition, going all the way back to the early Fathers of the Church, has always understood Our Lady's question to imply that she had already been inspired by the Holy Spirit to consecrate her virginity to God. If this were not the case, and she was intending to have marital relations with Saint Joseph after their solemn engagement ended and they lived together as husband and wife, then it logically follows that she would have assumed this was how she would conceive as the angel had foretold. Thus, her question would make no sense. Therefore, Our Lady's question can only be logically interpreted to mean: "Not only have I not had marital relations with St. Joseph during this time of our solemn engagement, but even after our marriage I will not have marital relations with him." We may then conclude that Our Lady is here, not only stating the fact that she is a virgin at that moment, but also that she is determined to remain a virgin always.

The Meaning of Our Lady's Perpetual Virginity

Consecrated virginity was unknown in the Old Testament. It was an aspect of that "celibacy for the sake of the Kingdom of Heaven"(cf. Mt 19:10-12) which Jesus taught for those who were willing to accept it in the New Testament. Our Lady was no doubt inspired to her perpetual virginity by the light of the Holy Spirit. Her sinlessness and overwhelming holiness allowed her such an openness to the inspirations of the Holy Spirit that she not only recognized virginity consecrated to God as a spiritual treasure, but also she steadfastly consecrated her own virginity to God. Saint Thérèse of Lisieux, a Doctor of the Church, was of the opinion that if Our Lady could only become the Mother of Jesus by breaking her vow of virginity to God, she would not have become Jesus' Mother. The Little Flower was convinced that Our Lady would never take back what she had already given to God.

Church historians point out that the doctrine of Mary's

perpetual virginity was to become an ideal for many Christian men and women who wanted to give their lives more fully to Christ. Thus, the ideal of consecrated celibacy in both the priesthood and religious life found support in the model of the Virgin Mary. Unfortunately, after Vatican Council II, some liberal Catholic theologians, in an air of theological ferment within the Church at the time, began to reinvestigate long accepted truths with an attitude of complete freedom, as if they were not defined Church teachings. Thus, the perpetual virginity of Our Lady, accepted as dogma for over fifteen centuries since the first Lateran Council (A.D. 649), began to be questioned and rejected by some within the Church. Could it not be that, in the social climate of the late 1960's and the 1970's, when Western culture was experiencing the devastating effects of the so-called "Sexual Revolution" and some Catholics were promoting a "new sexual morality" that was nothing but a distortion of authentic Catholic moral teaching, that certain people rejected the teaching and example of Our Lady's perpetual virginity because it was a moral rebuke to the sexual license they were spreading? As Ven. Archbishop Fulton J. Sheen put it, "No one becomes a heretic for the way they want to think, but for the way they want to live."

The late Archbishop, a great devotee of Our Lady, also used to say: "Where a devotion to the Blessed Virgin Mary is strong, womanhood, motherhood and purity are all held in great respect!" Devotion to the Virgin Mary is a strong bulwark against the sins of the flesh! If it is rejected, the road to sexual promiscuity would open even wider.

Consecrated or perpetual virginity, embraced publicly or privately, is an outstanding sign of the virtue of purity. This is why the sex-crazed society we live in not only rejects it, but attacks it viciously. This author remembers hearing slogans during the turbulent 60's and 70's like "Down with virginity." In the same way, we hear constant demands, both from inside and outside the Church, that priestly celibacy be done away with. Since the perpetual virginity of Our Lady is a model and encouragement for consecrated celibacy, it is no wonder it has been the object of much blasphemy, which we counter by our First Saturday Devotions of reparation.

Virginity, seen as the chastity lived by young people before marriage, is another important expression of this virtue. Today, many teenagers are ridiculed by their peers if they admit that are still "virgins." It has become a widespread assumption that every teenager is "sexually active." Thank God and Our Lady that this is not so. Many young people recognize that their gift of sexuality is meant to be a special gift reserved for married life. They struggle hard to maintain their virginity before marriage. Today, we must encourage young people to look to the Virgin Mary as their example and to seek her protection with their prayers. There are also a few clever little reminders that help, too. One is a "chastity ring," worn to remind young people to say "I don't" before they say "I do." Another is a chastity button that says, "I'm worth waiting for."

The Virgin Mary is a great support to all of us in our practice of purity according to our state in life. No wonder the world blasphemes her perpetual virginity. Let us make reparation for these blasphemies. In this way, we will win through the intercession of the Immaculate Heart of Mary greater graces for purity for the virtuous to remain faithful and for those whose lives have been caught up in sexual chaos, to return to the Divine Mercy of Jesus.

The Five First Saturdays Devotion
Reparation for Blasphemies Against
Mary's Divine Motherhood

Belief in Mary as the Mother of God is one of the most cherished beliefs of Catholics. This privilege of Our Lady is the basis and reason for all the other privileges she received from God. It was precisely because she was chosen from all women to be the Mother of Jesus Christ, the Son of God who took His human nature from her, that she was conceived without Original Sin (the privilege of her Immaculate Conception); that she remained a virgin before, during and after the birth of Jesus (the privilege of her Perpetual Virginity); that she played a very special part with Jesus in His mission of redeeming the world (her privilege as Co-Redemptrix); and that she was assumed body and soul into Heaven when her earthly life was ended (the privilege of her Assumption).

It was only fitting that Our Lady enjoy all of these privileges in order to fulfill her exalted vocation from God. After all, if we could have chosen our own earthly mother and then be allowed to give her the choicest blessings to make her the best of mothers, would we not have done so? Then how much more would Jesus do that, since He in fact did choose His own Mother, and then endow her with all those gifts that would make her the very best of all mothers!

The Mother of God

It is very important to clarify at this point exactly what we mean, as well as what we do not mean, when we call Mary "the Mother of God." Let us start with what we do not mean. When we call Our Lady "the Mother of God," we do not mean she gave birth to Jesus in His Divinity. Many people, especially among our separated brethren, are often under this grave misunderstanding. As God, the Second Divine Person existed from all eternity. That means He had no beginning, and He will never have an ending. If Mary gave birth to Jesus in His Divinity, then that would mean that Jesus is not God, since God could not have a beginning. It would also make Our Lady appear that she was some sort of "super-goddess" which she is absolutely not.

What, then, do we mean when we call Mary "the Mother of God"? To try to explain this simply but clearly, we must use two words taken from philosophy. They are "nature" and "person." Nature describes the makeup of something, with all its powers and abilities. Nature answers the question: "What is it?" For example, it can be an angel, a man or woman, an animal or even God.

Spiritual Natures

Each of these has the powers and abilities that are part of their nature. God, by His Divine Nature, has infinite knowledge and power, and can create things out of nothing. No other nature, because it is created and limited, has the powers of God's Nature. An angel, by his angelic nature which is totally spiritual, has vast infused knowledge and power and can do many things human beings cannot. Men and women, by their human nature which is partly spiritual (their soul) and partly material (their body), have the ability to reason with their intellect and to freely choose with their wills, along with the abilities that come from their bodily powers, such as the use of the senses, movement and reproduction. Animals, whose nature is purely material, have the ability to use senses, move about and reproduce their species, but they lack the human being's ability to reason intellectually and to choose freely. They are governed largely by instinct.

"Person" refers to any being having intelligence and free will, one who is responsible for his/her actions and the consequences of them. We refer to the "person" as the "agent" or the one who acts through the powers of his/her nature. Person answers the question, "Who is it?" It follows, then, that there are only three categories of "persons": a Divine Person, such as God the Father, an

189

angelic person, such as St. Michael; and a human person, such as Saint Thérèse. Animals, because they lack the ability to reason intellectually and to choose freely, are not "persons" in this philosophical sense.

Divine Nature of Jesus

Let us apply these ideas of "nature" and "person" to Jesus, and therefore to why we call Mary, His Mother, "the Mother of God." What the Catholic Church teaches as her defined dogma is that in Jesus there are two natures (one Divine and the other human), but only one Person (the Second Divine Person of the Blessed Trinity). From all eternity, without beginning and without end, Jesus was the Second Divine Person, with His Divine Nature which He possesses with God the Father and God the Holy Spirit. He had the same infinite powers to create, to redeem and to sanctify as They did.

What happened in the moment of the Incarnation was that this Second Person, while keeping His Divine Nature, also took a human nature. He did this by taking His flesh and blood from the womb of the Virgin Mary, when the power of the Holy Spirit came upon her to accomplish this greatest event in human history. As we profess in the Apostles' Creed: "He (Jesus) was conceived by the Holy Spirit, born of the Virgin Mary ..." Though Jesus has a human consciousness, a human intelligence and a human free will, He is not a human person. Rather, the Second Divine Person now acts through human nature He acquired from Our Lady. In other words, the "agent" responsible for acting through the human nature of Jesus is a Divine Person.

The Motherhood of Mary

Now, let us apply all this to Our Lady's title of "Mother of God." A human mother is always the mother of a person. Although the mother and father together conceived the child, and God alone infused the soul into the child at the moment of conception (which is why we respect all human life from the moment of conception), the mother is called the mother of the whole person. For example, we say: "This is John's mother" or "This is Anne's mother." We do not say, "This is the mother of John's body" or "This is the mother of Anne's body." Motherhood always applies to a person. And the only person in Jesus Christ, who is fully God and fully man, is the Second Divine Person. Therefore, since Mary is the Mother of Jesus' human nature, we can say of her: "Mary is the Mother of Jesus," "Mary is the Mother of One Who is a Divine Person," "Mary is the Mother of God!"

This teaching of the Catholic Church was declared in a special way at the ecumenical Council of Ephesus in 431 A.D. (Ephesus is located in modern Turkey. A strong Catholic tradition says that St. John the Beloved, who received Our Lady into his care at the foot of the Cross, later in a time of persecution took her to Ephesus where there was a large Christian community. It was there that some say Our Lady was assumed into Heaven. It is still a site of Christian pilgrimage). At the time, some Christians had asked Nestorius, then Patriarch of Constantinople, if Mary could be called in Greek, "Theotokos," which meant literally the "God-bearer," or "Mother of God." The Patriarch answered that Mary could not be called "Theotokos," but only "Christotokos, the bearer of Christ," implying that in Jesus there was a human person (Christ) as well as a Divine Person (the Second Divine Person).

This teaching became the heresy we call "Nestorianism" after its founder. It undermined the whole reality of the Incarnation. What it implied was that God did not really become man, but He simply entered into union with a human person and coexisted there. Thus, according to this heresy, in Jesus of Nazareth there would have been a Divine Person with a Divine Nature, as well as a human person with a human nature. Furthermore, since the "agent" working in the human nature of Jesus would be only a human person, his actions would have had only limited merit. Only a Divine Person can perform an action of infinite merit. So, if only a human person (Christ) died on the Cross, the merit of His death would mean that all of us would still be in our sins, because a purely human person could not atone for our sins. However, when we maintain the true Catholic teaching that the only Person in Jesus was a Divine Person, then His dying on the cross would be meritorious to redeem the whole world! The Council of Ephesus, led by St. Cyril of Alexandria, condemned the heretical teaching of Nestorious and proclaimed Our Lady as "Theotokos," the "God-bearer" or "the Mother of God." The Christians of Ephesus were so overjoyed that they held a night-long procession throughout the streets of Ephesus chanting. "Theotokos! Theotokos!" It is our same joy to proclaim Mary as the "Mother of God!"

It is one of the intentions for the Five First Saturdays of the month to make reparation for those who, whether from misunderstanding or from deliberate disbelief, deny or ridicule or blaspheme this very special Catholic teaching about Our Blessed Mother. As she herself, inspired by the Holy Spirit, proclaimed in her great song of thanksgiving, her "Magnificat: From this day all generations will call me blessed; the Almighty has done great things for me, and holy is His Name!"

THE FIVE FIRST SATURDAYS DEVOTION
REPARATION FOR BLASPHEMIES BY THOSE WHO ALIENATE CHILDREN FROM DEVOTION TO OUR LADY

The Gospel records the story of the day that a group of mothers was approaching Jesus with their little children, in order for Him to place His hands on them and bless them. The disciples mistakenly thought that the children were at best a distraction to Our Lord, and at worst an annoyance that He did not want or need. After all, that was the attitude that the Pharisees, the acknowledged religious leaders of the day, had toward children. So they were stopping the mothers and children from approaching Jesus, turning them away. Our Lord's response was quick and clear: "Let the children come to Me, and do not prevent them; for the kingdom of heaven belongs to such as these." "After He placed His hands on them, He went away" (Mt 19:14-15).

Speak Often of Mary to the Children

It is clear from this incident how much Our Lord wants children to come to Him! From their earliest years, the young must be taught about Jesus, about His life, death and resurrection, about His Church, emphasizing her doctrine and Sacraments. This includes in a very special way the Church's rich treasury of teaching and devotion about the Blessed Virgin Mary. She is Jesus' mother, and must therefore be loved, honored and respected along with Him. She is also our mother, given to us by Jesus Himself from the Cross of Calvary: "Woman, behold your son!...Behold your mother" (Jn 19:26-27). And is there anything more instinctive than for a little child to seek his or her mother?

Even from a child's earliest years, he or she can begin to grasp a love for Our Lady in keeping with his or her stage of development. Please allow me to illustrate with an example drawn from my own family's experience that involves a niece of mine. This particular niece would often visit one of her uncles, who had a statue of Our Lady in his backyard. My family would often observe her standing for long periods of time in front of the statue, seemingly engrossed in an animated conversation with the Blessed Mother. One can only imagine what passed between the Immaculate Heart of Our Lady and the innocent heart of a child.

Silence about Our Lady

The foundation of Marian devotion should ordinarily be given in the home. Word and example must go together to assure that it will have a lasting effect. When children hear and see that Our Lady is important to their parents, she becomes important to them also. Many parents today, wanting to adopt what they mistakenly believe is a certain "broad-mindedness" about religious truths, take the attitude that they will not teach their children anything specific about religion. They say, "I will let my children grow up, and then they can make up their own minds about what they want to believe or not." (You will notice that they do not allow these same children to make up their own minds about whether they want to go to school or not!)

For a child to wait until he or she grows up to learn basic truths such as those of religion will be too late. The fallacy in this thinking is that to say nothing, is in effect to say something. The human mind at birth is what philosophers would call a "tabula rasa," that is, "a blank sheet." To have any knowledge in the mind, it must come either through experience or by teaching. Therefore, to say nothing about religious truths in this case Our Blessed Mother is to deprive the child of even knowing she exists. After all, you can only come to know the existence of another person when you have been introduced to them, whether by teaching about them, such as when we study about people from history, or by a personal encounter with that individual. Silence on the part of parents conveys to the child either that Our Lady does not exist, or that she is not very important. At the same time, silence on such important religious truths leaves a kind of intellectual vacuum which will very likely, sooner or later, be filled with erroneous ideas and false moral values. These may come from distorted teachings, the lure of passion which youth experience, or the negative influence of scandal, which Jesus said is unavoidable (cf. Mt 18:7). Left to itself, our fallen human nature tends to follow the law of gravity: it gets pulled down, not up. What lifts us up and strengthens us to resist the downward pull to immorality is God's grace working through the truths of our Catholic Faith.

Now, if these same parents speak about the Blessed Mother, especially with a sense of joy, enthusiasm and importance, this is bound to make a deep impact on the child. I have always believed that the initial faith of a child is actually a participation in the faith of the parents, or of other significant people in their lives, such as grandparents, godparents and teachers. With time, the children will make this participated faith their own personal faith.

What Keeps Children from Our Lady?

Through the First Five Saturdays Devotion, we make reparation for this failure to teach children about the Blessed Mother, due to neglect on the part of parents or others charged with their education. Worse still, however, are those who deliberately sow the seeds of indifference, disrespect, aversion and even contempt for the Blessed Mother. This can result from a number of motives. One would be a religious attitude or prejudice that mistakenly sees Our Lady as one who keeps us from Jesus. They argue that we must go to Jesus directly, and not to Jesus through Mary. But how can the one through whom Jesus came into the world, and whose last recorded words in Sacred Scripture are, "Do whatever He tells you" (Jn 2:5), ever possibly keep us from Jesus? In our reparation here, we should pray that such persons, who may be quite sincere despite their mistaken idea, may come to see that Mary is an open gate, not a locked door, on the sure path leading to Jesus!

Radical feminists also oppose love and esteem of Our Lady for themselves and others because, as we have seen in previous reflections, they reject certain essential elements of true feminism, namely, virginity and motherhood. They reject virginity because they want no limits on the promiscuous and often perverted sexual freedom they champion. Motherhood is rejected because it contradicts their desire for pleasure without responsibility. Radical feminists fail to see virginity as a precious gift by which youth, before marriage, preserve the gift of their sexuality for the person with whom they will share a lifelong union of love in marriage. They also reject motherhood, the very glory of womanhood, namely, her right through union with her husband to cooperate with God in bringing new life into the world. In contrast, Our Lady is honored by her faithful children as Virgin and Mother, and as such she is held up as an example for young people. So, as Virgin and Mother, Mary has become for radical feminists an object of distorted teaching, ridicule and even contempt and blasphemy. In their attempts to spread their agenda, they seek to poison the minds and hearts of young people against the Mother of God. After all, their mentality is prevalent in our secularized Western society. The consequence is much like breathing-in badly polluted air: it will eventually make one sick. Thus, radical feminist thought has infiltrated the thinking of many Catholic parents and educators, and in turn, like a contagious disease, has been transmitted to a large segment of our Catholic youth, who either do not know Our Lady or are prejudiced against her.

In responding to Our Lord's request to Sister Lucia at Pontevedra, Spain, for reparation for those who turn the young against His Mother, we must beg the graces needed for the conversion of hearts so rooted in such contempt for Our Lady. Because she is in glory in Heaven, Our Lady cannot directly suffer. But she "suffers" in the sense that she is deprived of the love of many of her young spiritual children on earth. Furthermore, if Jesus said it would be better for a person who scandalizes even one little one of God to have a millstone tied around his neck and be cast into the sea (cf. Mt 18:6), what punishment will await those who deliberately scandalize many little ones by turning them against God's own Mother? We must earnestly pray and offer sacrifices for them, that they may not be lost.

A Bitter Spiritual Battle Rages

There is a veritable battle between good and evil, light and darkness, going on in the world today. It has always existed, but it seems to have reached epidemic proportions in today's society. This can be especially seen in the struggle to win over the minds and hearts of the young. We saw this with the terrible "isms" of the 20th century. Communism broke up families by separating little children from their parents at the tenderest ages, so as to prevent proper moral guidance and religious training by parents, especially in a deeply religious country like Russia. Nazism boasted of its "youth camps" where young people were systematically subjected to an indoctrination that rejected God and glorified a "super race," only to have it end in catastrophic destruction in the world. This spirit is still found today in our post-Christian, secularized society. The media bombard the young with false and immoral values. Just imagine the negative

198

moral effects of MTV on youth, not only in America, but also throughout the world! Lately, even diplomats, such as those in the United Nations, have tried to gain control of the young under the guise of legislating "young peoples' rights." These laws are nothing more than attempts to separate children from parental authority and protection. They would leave children helplessly exposed to all kinds of exploitation by unscrupulous adults.

The Church, led by Saint John Paul II, is well aware of this unrelenting struggle and its importance. Both sides know that whoever controls the minds and hearts of the young controls the key to the future. The Holy Father, as a young priest in his native Communist-dominated Poland, untiringly reached out to the young to save the nation from embracing atheism. Even despite his poor health, he continued the same approach for the Universal Church through his World Youth Days of prayer. We, too, will assist in this struggle as we carry out the Five First Saturdays Devotion, making reparation for the evil done to our young people and winning the graces of conversion for them as well as for those who attempt to keep them from coming to Jesus through His Mother!

THE FIVE FIRST SATURDAYS DEVOTION
REPARATION FOR BLASPHEMIES BY THOSE WHO DISHONOR OUR LADY IN HER SACRED IMAGES

Art plays a very important part in the life of any society. In its many forms, such as painting, writing and music, the purpose of art is to give expression to the values, the beauty and the aspirations that men and women treasure in their hearts. Art can express a variety of sentiments from joy to sorrow, hope to disappointment, love to loneliness, even reverence to disrespect. It is one of the primary means by which people of a given generation form and express their culture.

The Powerful Influence of Religious Art

Religious art stands out among all these expressions because it touches the most profound and sacred sentiments we have, namely, those stemming from our relationship with God. Such art helps us to feel a sense of the presence of God and, in turn, moves us to pray more ardently and trust more confidently in His love and providential care. Devout people instinctively know this by their experience.

The Catholic Church has always used art as a part of her mission of evangelization. In past centuries, when most of the faithful were illiterate, they would learn much about their Catholic Faith by looking at artistic representations of events in Sacred Scripture. Scenes from the life of Christ, such as those depicting His birth, public life, death and resurrection, were extremely popular. They made these events of salvation very real and meaningful for these people of simple faith. The same effect continues today when religious art reinforces what a more educated faithful have already studied about the Faith. As Saint John Paul II wrote in his letter to artists in 1999, "In order to communicate the message entrusted to her by Christ, the Church needs art!"

Sacred art is also important for maintaining our sense of piety or religious devotion. This touches on a point that many non-Catholics often misunderstand. Catholics do not worship statues or holy pictures or any other images of Jesus or Our Lady or the saints. We have these representations just as ordinary people have photos of loved ones or statues of national heroes. They know that the photos or the statues are not the actual people being portrayed by them. But these images remind them of people they love and admire. Catholics use their sacred images to remind them of those whom they love deeply, namely, the Lord, His Blessed Mother, and the Saints.

The Image of Our Lady in Christian Art

Among the most popular images of Catholic art are those of Our Blessed Lady. Without a doubt, the theme of the Madonna and Child has inspired some of the most beautiful expressions created by human artists. Even the United States Post Office, despite objections of certain civil libertarians, issues its special stamp of the Madonna and Child every Christmas to meet popular demand.

Special representations of Our Lady have become part of the Catholic culture in various countries and even internationally, including Our Lady of Perpetual Help (Italy), Our Lady of Czestochowa (Poland), Our Lady of Pilar (Spain), Virgin Mary of Vladimir (Russia), Our Lady of Walsingham (England) and Our Lady of Loreto (Italy). Over the years it was Catholic devotion to Our Lady in these images that preserved a remnant of Catholic culture and identity, especially in times when the Church faced persecution from without and indifference from within.

Devotion to Our Lady through her images has also flourished in connection with places where she has appeared to various members of the faithful over the centuries. Names like Fatima (Portugal), Lourdes and Rue du Bac (France) and Knock (Ireland) are but a few of such places all over the world where the faithful come to honor Our Lady at her shrines. These same faithful and many others keep her image in their homes as reminders of their love for her and of their need to pray to her to seek her motherly protection and intercession.

Dishonor to Our Lady's Image

Connected to these various images of Our Lady have been certain Marian devotions. These include honoring her joys and sorrows, praying her Rosary, wearing her Miraculous Medal as well as wearing the Brown Scapular she gave us as Our Lady of Mount Camel. So, when Catholics honor images of Our Lady, there is a considerable sense of piety involved. She is our spiritual Mother who cares for us, our protectress who defends us from all harm, physical and spiritual. Our intercessor with her Son, Jesus Christ. Therefore, whenever her image is dishonored in any way, it is an offense to devout Catholics because it is a serious dishonor to Our Lady and, consequently, to her Divine Son. It demands reparation for the affront given and intercession for God's mercy for those who cause it.

Causes for This Dishonor

Sometimes this dishonor is shown to Our Lady's images by destroying, mutilating, decapitating, spray painting, burning or in any other way disfiguring them. These are outrages that necessitate our reparation. Many times these things are done by members of occult groups who do them to express their contempt for God. Other times it may be the work of people who are violently angry at God for some distorted reason and who resort to desecration to convey that anger. Even very famous images of Our Lady have been disfigured over the centuries. For

203

example, the image of Our Lady of Czestochowa suffered desecration. This sacred image was thought to have been painted by Saint Luke on a table top made by Saint Joseph and used by the Holy Family at Nazareth. In 1430 a group of robbers attempted to rob this priceless image. They put it onto a wagon to carry it away, but the animals pulling the cart would not move. In desperation, the robbers tried to destroy the image with their swords, inflicting a couple of "wounds" on the face of Our Lady on the image. Interestingly, when certain monks charged with repairing the image later tried to cover the scars on Our Lady's face, the wounds only reappeared. Consequently still today the image bears those scars, reminding us of how much indignity is heaped upon Our Lady because she is our spiritual Mother!

Another equally outrageous dishonor to Our Lady in her images is to produce distorted images or make them from offensive materials. A blasphemous example of this appeared in an art gallery in Brooklyn, New York. The image of Our Lady was made of most offensive matter and covered with obscene items. Such outrage is certainly a product of the deliberate contempt and mockery fostered by the atheistic, perverted sub-culture that exists in much of our society today. Such desecrations are terribly offensive to the Lord Jesus because they seriously offend His Mother. No doubt the punishment for these sins will also be great. This is why we need first to make reparation for the offense to Our Lord and His Holy Mother by our loving honor of them, and then pray for those who would produce such disgraceful images.

A final form of dishonor to the images of Our Lady is to forbid them to be displayed for prayer and veneration. This can happen in private homes as well as parish churches. Many churches, remodeled after Vatican Council II, lost much of their religious art. If you walk into some of these churches today, they resemble stark meeting halls rather than places conducive to fervent prayer and worship. They became subject to what might be called a "neo-iconoclasm," a word stemming from the Greek word for "imagebreaking." In the 7th and 8th centuries, especially in the Eastern Church, there was an intense controversy over whether religious images could be used or not. Those who opposed their use said religious images were idols and so they destroyed them (thus the title "iconoclasts"). The Second Council of Nicea (787) finally defined that religious images were worthy of veneration and ordered them to be restored. After all, they had been a part of Christian worship since the earliest centuries of the Church, as paintings in the catacombs attest. In fact, one of the earliest known images of Our Lady is found on the wall of the Roman catacomb known as the cemetery of Saint Priscilla. Art experts estimate it dates back to about 175AD. It shows Our Lady seated, holding the Christ Child on her knee.

We Should Honor Our Lady's Images

We can see how important it is that we honor Our Lady for the dishonors shown her. This is our reparation. Then we must pray for those who have so tragically dishonored her, because they will face a severe judgement for such outrages. These are not always sins of weakness, but very often involve deliberate contempt. As we practice our devotion of the Five First Saturdays, we will be offering this important reparation and intercession. At the same time, we can do even more. We should have images of Our Lady in our own homes, to remind us of her presence, of her maternal love and care for our families.

We should pray before these images of the Mother of God. Especially when we gather with family members to pray her Rosary. You might also consider working with others to begin a parish or neighborhood "Pilgrim Virgin of Fatima" program, where the image of Our Lady will travel from home to home, or in the parish school from classroom to classroom. You will only know in Heaven how many you have helped come closer to the Mother of God and our Mother, too.

CHAPTER EIGHT

OUR LADY OF FATIMA'S MESSAGE AND
THE SPIRITUALITY OF SAINT PADRE PIO
SAINT PADRE PIO'S DEVOTION TO THE
IMMACULATE HEART OF MARY

What may appear to many to be a mere coincidence in
God's plan often has great significance. This very clearly appears to be the case with the apparitions of Our
Lady of Fatima and the great holiness and extraordinary mission of St. Padre Pio. The timing of the Blessed
Mother's apparitions and the stigmatization of St. Padre
Pio, undoubtedly the most significant mystical event of
his life, are nearly simultaneous. The Padre received the
"invisible stigmata" of the five wounds of Jesus in his
hands, feet, and side (i.e., he felt the pain but there were
no visible wounds) on September 20, 1915. Our Lady
made six appearances at Fatima on the 13th of each
month from May to October 1917. St. Padre Pio then re-

ceived the "visible stigmata" (i.e., the five wounds were clearly marked in his flesh) on September 20, 1918, the event that thrust him into an apostolic mission of world-wide influence.

Another consideration is that the spirituality of St. Padre Pio most strikingly embodies the Message of Our Lady of Fatima! We know that the Fatima Message has played a crucial part in God's plan for the peace and salvation of the world for nearly the past 100 years. We can, then, rightfully ask: Did God raise up St. Padre Pio to be an outstanding witness and example for living out the Fatima Message? A comparative study reveals remarkable parallels between the two. Allow me to focus on some elements of Our Lady's message for May and June, and see them in St. Padre Pio's life.

Accepted Co-redemptive Suffering in Reparation for Sins and for the Conversion of Sinners

Our Lady, on God's behalf, asks young Lucia, Jacinta, and Francisco: "Do you wish to offer up to God all the sufferings He desires to send you in reparation for the sins by which He is offended, and in supplication for the conversion of sinners?"

The children respond willingly, "Yes, we do!"

Our Lady then assures them they will have much to suffer, adding, however, "the grace of God will comfort you."

This kind of suffering is called "co-redemptive suffering," since it is joined to Jesus' suffering to make up for sins (reparation) and to obtain the grace of conversion for sinners. St. Paul describes this suffering clearly: "In
208

my own flesh I fill up what is lacking in the sufferings of Christ for the sake of His Body, the Church" (Col 1:24). We must carefully understand this teaching. There is nothing wrong, or missing, or lacking in what Jesus suffered. Rather, He wants us to share in His great work of redemption. In a similar way, for example, Jesus did not need the five loaves of the young boy to feed the crowd of over 5,000 (cf. Jn 6:1-13), but He chose to use the loaves the boy presented so generously.

St. Padre Pio, like the Fatima children, was generous in accepting "co-redemptive suffering" from the Lord. Part of the inscription on his First Mass holy card stressed his desire to offer himself as a "victim of Divine Love" to suffer with Jesus to win souls: "With You may I be for the world the way, the truth, and the life, and through You, a holy priest, a perfect victim!" In an ecstasy, he prayed to Jesus: "I want to help You ... lt grieves me to see You in this way (suffering from men's sins). Have they committed many offenses against You lately? Make it possible for me to help You with that heavy, heavy cross ... You are there ... what is there to fear?" (Diary, pp. 40-41).

As Our Lady promised the children that they would be comforted, St. Padre Pio knew the same. He wrote to his spiritual director, Padre Benedetto: "It is a happiness that the Lord gives me to rejoice almost only in suffering. In such moments, more than ever, everything in the world pains and annoys me, and I desire nothing except to love and to suffer. Yes, my (spiritual) father, in the midst of all these sufferings I am happy because I feel my heart throb in unison with the Heart of Jesus" (Letters 1, p. 194).

Devotion to the Immaculate Heart of Mary

In the June apparition the children ask if they will go to Heaven. Our Lady answers that Jacinta and Francisco will go soon, but that Lucia must remain for some time longer: "Jesus wishes to make use of you to make me known and loved. He wants to establish in the world devotion to my Immaculate Heart." Lucia then became saddened. Our Lady consoled her: "Do not be disheartened. I will never leave you ... My Immaculate Heart will be your refuge and the way that will lead you to God." Then Our Lady opened her hand, and an immense light came forth, enveloping the children and making them see themselves in God. In the front of the palm of Our Lady's right hand, there was a heart encircled with thorns which pierced it. The children understood this was the Immaculate Heart of Mary, wounded by the sins of humanity. Our Lady wanted people to make up for these sins by acts of love.

From early childhood, St. Padre Pio was devoted to Our Lady. He would call her affectionately, "Mammina," (my little Mother) or "Madonnina" (my little Lady). A little sign over the door of his room summed up how much Our Lady meant to him: "Mary is the inspiration (beginning) of my hope!"

St. Padre Pio was devoted to Our Lady under various titles. One was Our Lady of Libera, patroness of Pietrelcina, his birthplace. She had freed the city on various occasions from war, plague, and natural disasters. He, no doubt, learned to trust Our Lady in all his trials and concerns.

He also honored Mary as Our Lady of Grace; patroness

of the friary at San Giovanni Rotondo. He used to say that all the great graces of his life came to him through the intercession of Our Lady.

Finally, he was greatly devoted to the Immaculate Heart of Our Lady of Fatima. It was she who cured him miraculously in 1959 from an illness that had so weakened him that he was confined to bed for some time. Afterwards, he venerated a special statue of her sent to him by the bishop of Fatima, and he always made his thanksgiving after Mass at the foot of that statue.

Just as little Lucia was assured of Our Lady's constant protection and consolation, St. Padre Pio enjoyed the same. When a friar once asked him "Padre Pio, does Our Lady ever come to your room?" he answered, "Why don't you ask me if she ever leaves?"

Ardent Appeal to Pray the Rosary

In both apparitions (May and June), Our Lady asked that the Rosary be prayed. In May, she told of the power of the Rosary: "Pray the Rosary every day, in order to obtain peace for the world and the end of the war." She added that Francisco would have to pray many Rosaries before he could go to Heaven. In June, Our Lady told Lucia: "I want you to pray the Rosary every day ..."

St. Padre Pio is certainly known for his love of the Rosary. When he was old and feeble, he needed the help of some friars to get dressed in the morning. As he was dressing one day, he told Padre Alessio, "Get me my weapon!" Startled, Padre Alessio responded, "Weapon? Padre Pio, you don't have a weapon." St. Padre Pio answered, "Get me my Rosary!" The Rosary was his weapon to do good and defend against evil.

St. Padre Pio learned to pray the Rosary many times a day as a young novice, a practice that increased with time. One day a man bragged to St. Padre Pio, "I have said the Rosary five times today."

Padre responded, "That's very good! I have said about thirty-five Rosaries!"

The man could not believe that and asked, "Padre Pio, how could you have said thirty-five Rosaries? You have been busy all day long."

The Padre answered, "You do one thing at a time; I do three or four things at a time."

A final quote of St. Padre Pio sums up his response to Our Lady's request for the Rosary, and why he always urged others to pray it often: "Is there any prayer more beautiful or more pleasing than the one Our Lady taught us herself? More beautiful than the Rosary? Always pray the Rosary!"

The apparitions of Our Lady of Fatima in the months of July and August stand in great contrast.

The apparition of July 13, 1917 occurred at the usual apparition site of the Cova da Iria and was considerably longer than all the other apparitions except that of October.

During this apparition a number of things were revealed that became parts of the "three secrets" of Fatima. Actually, it might be more accurate to say that there was only one secret, all revealed in this July apparition, but with three parts. But, not to cause confusion, we will simply

213

refer to them as "three secrets." These three messages will be the main focus in our present reflection.

The August apparition, on the other hand, did not occur like all the other apparitions on the 13th of the month, nor did it occur in the Cova. Rather, certain anticlerical government officials, bent on disturbing the apparitions, deceptively kidnapped the visionaries and imprisoned them in a jail in the neighboring city of Ourém.

As a result, the anticipated apparition never happened that day. However, Our Lady suddenly appeared without warning to the visionaries on August 19th (or 15th) at a place called Valinhos, located a short distance from their homes. This unexpected visit was quite brief, but it reinforced the basic Message of Our Lady for prayer and penance for the eternal salvation of souls.

Reminders

As we compare Our Lady's Message for July and August with the spirituality of St. Padre Pio, we must realize that Our Lady repeated many requests in these apparitions that she had already made in May and June. As St. John Paul II is quoted as saying, "We do not need a whole lot of new ideas, just a lot of reminders!" So Our Lady often gently reminded her children—Lucia, Francisco and Jacinta, and all of us through them—of the main points of her Message, so that we would remember to carry them out very faithfully.

Let us now consider the main points of Our Lady's July and August Messages, and see how St. Padre Pio also lived these out faithfully.

Hell

One of the most powerful experiences the young visionaries had throughout the course of Our Lady's apparitions was the vision of Hell. This unforgettable vision constitutes the "first secret" of Fatima because the children, directed by Our Lady, would not talk about it initially except among themselves. It was only publicly revealed later on in the memoirs of Sister Lucia written years afterwards.

God chose to let the visionaries see Hell. It undoubtedly left a lasting impression on them. Here is a part of Lucia's description of what the children saw:

"They saw a sea of fire. Plunged in this fire were demons and souls that looked like transparent embers, some black or bronze, in human form, driven about by the flames that issued from within themselves, together with clouds of smoke. They were falling on all sides, just as sparks cascade from great fires, without weight or equilibrium, amid cries of pain and despair which horrified us so that we trembled with fear ..."

Even for these privileged souls, the vision was extremely frightful. What consoled and preserved them through it was that Our Lady had already told them in her May apparition that they were all going to Heaven.

Hell is a reality: it exists! But it is something most people would not care to think about, much less see, because it means admitting even the possibility of going there. Our Lady herself summed up the impact of this vision when she said kindly but sadly to the children: "You have seen Hell where the souls of poor sinners go."

As mentioned above, Our Lady in her earlier apparitions had already requested prayers and sacrifices for the conversion and salvation of souls. But by showing the children Hell, with its grave, unending torments, Our Lady emphasized how urgent and essential was the task of saving souls. The children realized graphically the tragic consequences that awaited any soul that would be lost.

In her brief August apparition, Our Lady again stressed the importance of offering prayers and sacrifices for the conversion of sinners. She said to the children with a sad expression:

"Pray, pray very much and make sacrifices for sinners, for many souls go to Hell because they have nobody to pray and make sacrifices for them."

According to Lucia's memoirs, Jacinta was the one most struck by this urgent Message. The notion of an eternity of suffering affected her greatly. She became extremely zealous in saving souls from Hell by her constant prayer and sacrifices, such as giving her lunch to hungry children or bearing with thirst as a sacrifice.

Saint Padre Pio

St. Padre Pio understood the importance of Hell as a deterrent to sin, especially mortal sin which, if unrepented, would land a person in Hell. A story is told of a man who came to Confession to him who was living a life of mortal sin. St. Padre Pio told the man, "You had better change your life, or you will end up in Hell."

The man answered, "Padre Pio, I don't believe in Hell." St. Padre Pio answered the man, "Well, you will when you get there!" St. Padre Pio was only too aware of the sufferings of Hell.

In another situation, a widow kept asking him if her husband, who had died recently, was in Heaven. At first, St. Padre Pio would not answer her. Finally, as she insisted, he told her, "I cannot bear to see your husband in Hell, he is so horrible looking. Although he had made a Confession shortly before he died, he deliberately withheld confessing that he had committed adultery, and so he died unrepentant with these grave sins on his soul."

Victim for Souls

In our previous reflection for the May and June apparitions of Our Lady, we touched on St. Padre Pio's great desire to be a "victim" with Christ for the salvation of souls. Here, let us add a powerful statement of his, clearly showing his ardent longing that no soul be lost: "My Jesus, I want to be a victim for others. Punish me and not others, under the condition that I love you and everyone is saved." This is no doubt the reason he spent himself in the work of the confessional, hearing Confessions for over fifteen hours a day when he was younger. It was estimated that he heard over five million Confessions in his lifetime. Why? That sins may be forgiven, and everyone saved! Yet, the fear of Hell should not be the primary focus of our Christian life; rather, it must be our sincere love for God and for one another. However, fear of Hell, like a safety net, can halt us from mortal sin when love itself may not yet be a strong enough motive. Even St. Dismas, the "good thief," knew its importance when he asked his fellow thief who was resisting repentance even

217

in the very last moments of his life, "Have you no fear of God?" (cf. Lk 23:40). Hell is one of the "four last things" along with death, judgement, and Heaven. St. Augustine once said that if we meditate daily on these "four last things," we would never commit a mortal sin.

Of all the apparitions of Our Lady of Fatima in the Cova da Iria, the last two combined what appear to be the most simple (September) and the most spectacular (October) of them all. As we have seen, on August 13th there was no "public" apparition of Our Lady to the shepherd children, Lucia, Francisco, and Jacinta, because they had been abducted and imprisoned by disbelieving government officials.

Great crowds of people packed the roads leading to the

Cova in September and October. As a result, the visionaries had a difficult time getting to the apparition site. People would throw themselves on their knees before the children, and beg them to offer their petitions to Our Lady: "Heal my crippled son." "Cure my daughter who is deaf." "Let my husband and son return safely from the war." "Let Our Lady convert me, a poor sinner." "Ask Our Lady to cure my tuberculosis."

It seemed as if every kind of human need and suffering was being presented to Our Lady. This is a great example of how instinctively God's children turn to their Heavenly Mother in all their needs and sorrows.

We will now summarize Our Lady's message for these two months, and then compare it to the spirituality St. Padre Pio lived out in his own life.

The Rosary and Fatima

In all her apparitions, Our Lady requested the children to "pray the Rosary" or "continue to pray the Rosary." In fact, she specified that they pray the Rosary "every day." How pleasing this prayer is to Our Lady! She wants her children to pray it because it is such a powerful means of doing good and overcoming evil in our daily lives.

Furthermore, it helps us to pray more deeply and more personally by teaching us to combine "formal prayer" and "mental prayer." In formal prayer we use word formulas composed by others to guide us in how to speak to God, in what to say to Him. In the Rosary, we recite the Our Father (the Prayer Our Lord Himself taught us), the Hail Mary, the Glory be, the Apostles' Creed, and the Hail, Holy Queen. We then add "mental prayer" to these

220

inspiring word-formulas. This happens when we reflect or meditate on the various mysteries of the life (Joyful Mysteries), light (Luminous Mysteries), death (Sorrowful Mysteries) and resurrection (Glorious Mysteries) of Our Lord, mysteries in which Our Lady also plays a prominent part. By reflecting on the simple events in these mysteries, we get to know Jesus and Mary much better, indeed, in a very personal way. This, no doubt, helps to advance us in our spiritual lives.

The Rosary and Saint Padre Pio

We have already seen St. Padre Pio's great love for the Rosary. He himself prayed it many times a day. What better proof could there be to show how much importance he put on its daily recitation. He used to say that Our Lady herself gave us the Rosary. And why? Because he knew Our Lady was teaching us by it to grow daily in faith, hope, and love, and all the other basic virtues of the Christian life.

We can only imagine how much St. Padre Pio loved Our Lady under her title of "Our Lady of the Rosary." He became one of the most successful salesmen for her Rosary, always encouraging his "spiritual children," all who came to him, and all who sought his assistance to pray the Rosary daily! He knew how effectively the Rosary moved Our Lord, with and through the intercession of His Blessed Mother, to bestow great graces on His people. Our Lady herself told the shepherd children that by praying the Rosary, souls could be saved from going to Hell, wars could be stopped, and peace could be given to the world. After the Holy Sacrifice of the Mass, our Catholic people feel a special attraction and power in the recitation of the Rosary. We can only imagine how many souls St. Padre Pio saved from Hell, and how much other good he must have done by his daily recitation of many Rosaries. The prayer beads could often be seen passing quietly through his fingers.

The Miracle of the Sun

It was estimated that about 75,000 people had come from near and far for the October apparition because Our Lady had promised Lucia that she would work an undeniable miracle to prove to the people that the apparitions were indeed real. Many devout believers came to pray and honor Our Lady and see a sign of God's love and glory. Others were hardened disbelievers, atheists and agnostics – who came to scoff at any idea of a miracle or, at least, wondering with great hesitancy whether anything at all would happen.

Well, something quite spectacular did happen. The sun began to "dance" in the sky, giving off bright colors that looked like a multi-colored fireworks display. People were mesmerized with wonder and awe! All of a sudden, the mood changed completely to one of overwhelming fear. The crowds saw the sun suddenly begin to hurtle down toward the earth. Many thought it was the end of the world. The earth seemed that it would be consumed in a flaming sun. Many fell to their knees, confessing their sins aloud. Even atheists began to believe and pray.

Suddenly, just before it seemed the sun would impact the earth, it began to recede and return to its normal place in the sky. But what startling effects followed. They were beyond imagination. Many infirm people—the blind, the crippled, and the like—were healed! Many sinners were converted! Hardened atheists became believers! Even the ground and the clothes of the people, which were saturated with rain for days, were perfectly dry! This was the undeniable "miracle" Our Lady had promised Lucia.

And undeniable it was. In fact, it was seen for about fifty miles around Fatima. It brought an appropriate fear of God's justice and punishment to those who needed to turn away from lives of sin, and a greater trust in God's goodness, mercy, and power to inspire those who already knew the Lord to grow closer to Him.

St. Padre Pio, in his great zeal for the salvation of souls, knew how to be God's faithful instrument to provide either a sense of fear or trust in Him, according to the person's need. As he would say, "I do not give candy to those who need strong medicine." One example of "fear" that comes to mind was when an unbelieving couple (both were Masons) came separately to him in Confession. They wanted to mock St. Padre Pio and the Sacrament of Penance by making a false confession of "sins" they merely made up for the occasion. They went to Confession separately, as he heard men's Confessions at certain times, and women's Confessions at other times. As each of them came to him in the confessional, he was inspired by God to read their hearts. Knowing their deceit, he stopped each one, and he began to tell each of them their real sins—what they were, when they committed them, and how often! Both of these people were so shaken with fear, that a few days later they both went back to St. Padre Pio, made sincere Confessions and changed their lives. Fear of God's justice is often necessary to touch the hardened hearts of big sinners.

Consolation and Joy

Many of the people at Fatima on October 13, 1917, experienced not only fear, but great consolation as well. These were the devout and simple who already believed and loved God in their hearts. They saw the power and majesty of God in the "dance of the sun." They knew God has the whole world in His hands, including their lives. Consolation easily comes when we recall the saying: Nothing is going to happen to me today that God and I together can't handle!

St. Padre Pio knew how to encourage the faithful, even the weak and the fainthearted, and to give "candy" in the form of consolation when good people needed it. He would do this in his work in the confessional, in counseling his "spiritual children," and in responding to the literally thousands of people who wrote to him from all over the world. He often gave as advice something all of us would do well to remember: "Pray, hope, and don't worry!"

He would send the pilgrims to pray to Our Lady, or to visit the nearby shrine of St. Michael at Monte Sant' Angelo. He knew, like St. Francis to whom he was so greatly devoted, that the devil rejoices most when he can steal the joy out of the heart of a servant of God. On the other hand, the devil cannot harm the servant of God he sees filled with holy joy. St. Padre Pio was a true channel of God's joy and consolation to others, as Our Lady always is. We can sum up Our Lady's role in the prayerful words of (Mother) St. Teresa of Calcutta, who like St. Padre Pio was dedicated to Our Lady of Fatima and to her Rosary: "Immaculate Heart of Mary, Cause of Our Joy, pray for us!"

Our Lady of Fatima's Message and the Spirituality of Saint Padre Pio
Our Lady Cures Her Beloved Son

Two of my favorite photos of St. Padre Pio involve Our Lady of Fatima. In one, St. Padre Pio is praying devoutly before the Pilgrim Virgin statue of Our Lady of Fatima. At the base of the statue can be seen some white doves, a perfect symbol of the peace that no doubt filled that moment! The second photo shows St. Padre Pio bending over to kiss the feet of the Pilgrim Virgin.

Mother

These photos capture a very precious aspect of St. Padre Pio's life and holiness: his tremendous love for Our

Lady! He learned this love from his own mother Maria Giuseppa (Josephine) Forgione, whom the people of his home town of Pietrelcina warmly referred to as "Mamma Peppe!" From childhood, young Francesco Forgione developed a reverent trusting and tender love for Our Lady, calling her affectionately "Mammina" ("my little Mother") or "Madonnina" ("my little Lady"). After entering the Capuchin Order at Marcone in January 1903, as a novice, Fra Pio (Brother Pius, his religious name) learned to pray her Rosary many times daily, a practice he continued for the rest of his life, and encouraged others to do the same! His life on earth ended early on the morning of September 23, 1968 with the names of "Jesus" and "Mary" on his lips.

Marian Devotion

Throughout his life, St. Padre Pio honored the Blessed Virgin Mary under various titles. One was "Our Lady of Liberty," used by the people of Pietrelcina because she so often intervened to "liberate" or free them from war, plague and natural disasters. Another was "Our Lady of Grace," especially after going to San Giovanni Rotondo where the friary was named in her honor. He often prayed before her image in the chapel and always claimed that Mary's intercession was the source of all the great graces in his life.

Our Lady of Fatima

But the Marian title most closely connected with St. Padre Pio is Our Lady of Fatima. There are good reasons for this. St. Padre Pio received the visible stigmata (and a world-wide mission along with it) on September 20, 1918, while Our Lady appeared at Fatima from May 13 to October 13, 1917. The closeness of these events was no mere coincidence; they reflect God's timing! Mary's message of prayer, penance and co-redemptive love and sacrifice made a great impact on St. Padre Pio; in fact, it was to become his very life's work! This turned him profoundly to Our Lady of Fatima, and eventually entitled him to the role of "Spiritual Father of the Blue Army."

Severe Illness

There was to be one other great grace linking St. Padre Pio to Our Lady of Fatima with the deepest gratitude: Our Lady miraculously cured him! In April 1959, St. Padre Pio was forced to stay in bed for nine months with a severe illness which doctors diagnosed variously as bronchial pneumonia, pleurisy, and even a cancerous tumor requiring chemotherapy. As a result, he was unable to say Mass or hear confessions, a truly great cross for him. Rumors were spreading as far as the Vatican that St. Padre Pio was "deathly ill" with only a short time to live! During this same time, the Fatima Pilgrim Virgin statue was traveling throughout Italy. On August 5 the Pilgrim Virgin arrived by helicopter at San Giovanni Rotondo. Thousands of people came to pray and to honor her. On the next afternoon, the statue was placed in the sacristy for St. Padre Pio to venerate. He did so with great emotion, kissing the statue and placing a Rosary around it. But weakened and in pain, he had to be immediately carried back to his bedroom.

Miraculous Healing

Just before the helicopter carrying the Pilgrim Virgin took off, St. Padre Pio asked some friars who were with him, "Help me!" They helped him from his sickbed to the window in his room. The helicopter had just lifted off, circled the friary three times as a gesture of farewell to St. Padre Pio, and was beginning to fly north. Seeing the statue airborne, St. Padre Pio cried out: "My Little Mother, ever since you came to Italy, I had been laid low with sickness! Now that you are leaving, are you going to leave me this way?" Suddenly the helicopter swirled around and headed back toward the friary. The pilot later testified that he felt "compelled" to turn around. Then he saw St. Padre Pio at the window, crying out to Our Lady. Instantly, St. Padre Pio felt a mysterious force surge through his body. Then he leaped up and shouted, "I'm healed!" His cure was so complete that he was able to resume his full schedule of duties shortly after.

Bishop of Fatima

Whenever he spoke about this event, he called it a miraculous healing through Our Lady's intercession: "I prayed to the Madonnina, and the Madonnina healed me!" In gratitude, St. Padre Pio sent a crucifix to Bishop John Venancio, then Bishop of Fatima. In return, the Bishop had a special statue of Our Lady of Fatima made for St. Padre Pio, who received it as if it were Our Lady herself. Later, he had the statue placed over the vesting table in the sacristy. In this way, he could greet her as he went out to say Mass, and again on his return. Finally, at the feet of Our Lady of Fatima, under her watchful care, he devoutly made his thanksgiving after Mass every day!

OUR LADY OF THE ROSARY, PRAY FOR US.